GETTING
INTO
BROADCAST
JOURNALISM

GETTING
INTO
BROADCAST
JOURNALISM

A Guide to
Careers in
Radio and TV

GREGORY JACKSON

HAWTHORN BOOKS, INC.
PUBLISHERS / *New York*

Contents

1

What Is
This Book About?

Broadcast journalism is no place for the loner. Even the simplest broadcast news report is a group enterprise that comes on the air only with the contributions of many talents. There are the camera people, sound and lighting technicians, directors, producers, editors, reporters—an operation of many parts that must mesh together at high speed like the inside workings of a watch. These parts, of course, are people who perform *jobs*. The object of this book is to examine the many moving parts of a broadcast news operation and see how they interact.

What are the jobs? Just what does an assignment editor do? What's the difference between a broadcast news writer and a reporter? Where does the producer fit in? What talents do each of those jobs require? And what about beginning jobs? What are they, and who gets those jobs?

Also for the beginner there is the nitty gritty:

- What about schooling?
- What kind of early experience is best?
- Where does one start?

- What are the chances for women?
- What are the chances for minority group members?

That is what this book is about.

Broadcast journalism, however, cannot be divorced from the medium. It is still only a part of the much larger broadcast industry.

As a whole, the broadcast industry is a lot like the movie business. There are all kinds of people in it. There are wheeler-dealer producers and instant millionaires. There are artists and accountants. There's a place for the most highly specialized technician and the inexperienced mail room messenger. Tucked into all that is broadcast journalism. It may not belong there, cheek to cheek with the soap opera queens, the game show wizards, and the underarm deodorant commercials. But that's where it is.

Because of that, this book includes a discussion of how the industry works, who owns it, and who runs it. There's a chapter on the networks and local stations and how they do business with each other. And a look at the network and local station in terms of how it may affect the career of a young journalist.

There is also a discussion of the broadcast unions, which so quietly dominate the structure of television and radio. Sooner or later virtually all broadcast journalists will join a union or be required to work with union personnel in their specialties.

Many of the ways of broadcast journalism have become traditional, or at least customary, for those on the inside but are unknown to those on the outside. Even for the veteran in the industry, however, the trends of broadcasting are often mysterious, if not irrational.

Maybe that's what is so intriguing about a career in broadcast journalism. One never knows where one will end up. It's like setting off on a trip without being quite sure where one's going but suspecting it will be fun getting there.

This book, then, is written for young people who think they might want to get into radio and television news but don't really know what they're getting into, how to prepare for it, or where to start looking for a job. Reading this book won't get anybody a job in broadcasting—but it will help.

2

Is Journalism
for You?

Recently I talked with a young man who was terribly frus-
trated with what he was doing with his life, but he wasn't
sure what he could do about it. He was a friend of a friend
of mine who had asked me to meet the young man for lunch
and talk to him about a career in journalism. Nothing very
unusual. Virtually everyone in broadcast journalism is asked
the same kinds of questions by all kinds of young people. But
I think I got more out of this luncheon than my questioner,
for in the space of an hour's chat, it became clear to me what
was really bothering this fellow and, I suspect, thousands of
others like him.

He had recently graduated as an English major with high
marks from a reputable college. What he really enjoyed was
writing. That's what he wanted to do for a living. But he knew
nobody was going to pay him for a couple of years while he
tried to write a play or his first novel. He had done some work
on the college newspaper and he had liked that experience.
Journalism, it seemed to him, might be a logical choice. Now,
in talking to me, his concerns came down to two major questions: Did he have what it takes to become a journalist, and
what kind of credentials must he have—what kind of training
and background?

I couldn't answer the first question. In the period of an hour I could not judge whether he had the drive and the talent to make it. But the question about credentials was something else.

I told him that getting into journalism is not all that difficult. Doing well in it is very difficult. He was surprised. I told him that I did not mean to imply that there were news reporting jobs to be had just for the asking. I emphasized that the better the publication or the bigger the broadcast station, the harder it was to get hired. It takes a lot of work to find a job, but if he was willing to work hard enough and to take whatever kind of job was necessary to get in the door, he had enough credentials to get a job.

He was surprised, I guessed, because he had just come from college, where enormous emphasis is placed on professional, academic training. Classmates of his who wanted to become doctors were resigned to years of grinding study before they could even hope to claim the title. So, too, with the future engineers, architects, dentists, and so on.

Journalism, too, is a profession, he reasoned. It can bring fame and fortune and respect to at least some of its practitioners. How could he expect to succeed in it with merely a college degree in English? That was the underlying question that was really bothering him.

The fact is, most journalists start out with just enough credentials to get in the door. Where they go from there is another story. The major portion of a journalist's skill and knowledge comes through self-education. It comes through hard work and cultivating sources and keeping track of what's going on. It's a never-ending process. What ultimately determines success is the individual's personal drive, long-range ambition, and willingness to work at developing whatever natural talent one possesses.

That sounds fair enough, I suppose. But another fact is that probably more than half the people who go into journalism do not stay there. The number of famous *former* journalists in this country is quite remarkable. The list ranges from the late President John F. Kennedy to Ernest Hemingway. Alumni surveys at some of the best graduate schools of journalism reveal that more than half the students who start out in the news business quit and go into something else. The work may be directly related to the news business or only vaguely related to the communications industry. But for one reason or another, a large number sooner or later get out of the business of straight, "hard" news reporting. Why?

There is usually no single reason why anyone leaves a career. But when it comes to journalism, there are some rather broad areas one can explore for answers. And in exploring them, the young person considering a career in journalism may be better able to determine if it is a field for him or her.

Most obviously, journalism—particularly broadcast journalism—is a young person's game. It is demanding, exhausting, and competitively never-ending. One cannot rest on one's laurels. No matter how good one's story was yesterday, tomorrow is another day. At the age of twenty-five one can handle those eighteen hour days. But at fifty one doesn't answer with the same enthusiasm the 4:00 A.M. phone call telling of the latest riot that has to be covered.

There is also the question of job security. There isn't much of it in broadcasting. When it comes to hiring and firing, broadcast journalism is a lot like show business. Generally management can hire and fire producers and reporters as it pleases. There are always young people coming up, ready to work for less, nipping at the careers of those who got there before them but are tiring. For the young person eager to break in, that's good. For the older person anxious to hold a job, that can be a rather tense situation.

There is the fact of money. Good, established journalists are paid comfortable salaries, but they don't get wealthy. It has been my experience that journalists of all kinds never have any money. That probably has a lot to do with the kinds of people attracted to the field. They are not the banker types. Virtually all the network news superstars who make a great deal of money employ agents and money managers. Most of us, however, are not superstars, and at some point the fun of the job may be outweighed by the need to find a job that pays more money—and offers better job security.

There are, of course, many other reasons for giving up a career in journalism. Often it has to do simply with personality. To take one example, as a beginning journalist in the late 1940s, John Kennedy was covering the creation of the United Nations in San Francisco. The diplomats worked out the details of the UN charter behind closed doors. The news people were outside waiting to find out what the framers of the UN came up with. At that point the future president decided he would rather be on the inside making the deals than on the outside reporting on them. Kennedy's personality was just not designed for journalism. He had a flair for putting together programs. He had an instinct and a need for political power. The same kind of thing can be said of the successful manager climbing up the corporate ladder.

Generalities are always dangerous, but journalists very rarely are attracted to the corporate world. They are not interested in becoming managers or administrators responsible for the lives of hundreds or even thousands of other people beneath them. What journalists are interested in is the next good story.

That is not to say journalists are generally retiring types, observers standing on the sidelines and letting the rest of the world fight it out. A lot of being in the right place at the right time has to do with a willingness to *seize* the opportunity when it comes by. No one teaches that. The highly successful journalist inevitably *forced* himself or herself on the industry. For example, only rarely does the broadcast news industry go looking for someone to hire. The people who make it do so because they out-hustled the nearest competition. They are determined and ready to ask very difficult questions of the world about them. One usually associates that kind of personality with outgoing, bold kinds of people. It is true that outwardly, at least, many journalists are rather quiet, more observing than extroverted. But as a colleague of mine once put it, many of the best journalists are shy extroverts.

There is, then, no single kind of personality that characterizes the journalist, and there are no guarantees of success no matter what the preparation for a career in broadcast journalism. Success in broadcasting is relative, too. One need not work in the big city stations or at the network level to have fun, to enjoy the challenge of broadcast journalism. There probably isn't a network journalist alive who has not at some time or another looked back wistfully at the early years when he or she worked in the more casual atmosphere of a small, local station that was close to the community.

All young people face a problem in selecting a career. Rarely is such a process done alone. Almost always there is pressure from adults—parents, friends, advisors—who want to help avoid the anxiety of going from one job to another before finding the right one. Thus we can explain the perennial pressure on youngsters to become lawyers or doctors or dentists or engineers or teachers. Those jobs look safe, secure, and well-paid.

Broadcast journalism doesn't work that way, but there is a certain attraction connected with its uncertainties that is often overlooked. It is exhausting and demanding, but it is also fun and challenging. The journalist is in the center of the action, and that kind of involvement opens a number of horizons—that is, other job opportunities—if that becomes necessary or desirable.

Finally, there are the benefits to journalism's loose boundaries. If there are few prescribed courses of action open to insure success in the news business, there are also few entry barriers. The profession thrives on the talents and energy of young people. There was not time to really make that clear to the young man with whom I had lunch, but later I was struck by how similar my early circumstances were to his.

I use myself not as an example of a great success story but rather of a somewhat typical example of the ways writers can end up in journalism and the totally unexpected developments that can affect their careers.

I, too, graduated from college as an English major. I, too, discovered that there weren't many employers outside the campus gates looking for English majors. On the day of graduation I went to Boise, Idaho, where my parents were living. I didn't have the slightest idea of what I wanted to do, except I, too, wanted to write. I was recently married, however, and my father was no longer interested in supporting me.

Most of my journalist colleagues say they had a powerful interest in news reporting for as long as they can remember. Most of them started on a high school newspaper and continued working on one journalistic enterprise or another the rest of their early lives. I did not. But I wish that I had. It would have made my first years in the business a lot easier. I was always interested in writing, but I had spent my time writing fiction.

Home from college that first day, I took stock of my prospects and abilities. Business didn't interest me. I had had some experience as a salesman, but I didn't want to do that. My only criteria at that moment was that whatever I chose, it *had* to be fun. Salary was secondary. After a quick mental inventory I realized that all I was able to do (that somebody might pay me for) was type and write a grammatically correct sentence.

With that in mind I went to talk to the managing editor of the local newspaper. Because Boise was a rather small town in those days, the managing editor knew me slightly or knew my family or knew somebody I knew. I can't remember which it was right now. But he was sympathetic and we seemed to hit it off.

I must confess also that I lied shamelessly. I told him that I had worked on the college newspaper and that I had been interested in journalism all of my life.

Remarkably enough, he told me he would hire me as a cub reporter. But more remarkably, he told me of a colleague of his who was the bureau chief of United Press International in Boise. UPI paid more than he could, the managing editor said, and he sent me over to see the bureau chief.

When I got there, I lied not only about my journalistic background but also about my "close" friendship with the managing editor whom I had just met. As it turned out, the bureau chief was scheduled to go on vacation, but he was waiting for a summer relief man to fill out his small, three-person staff. The summer reliefer hadn't shown up. I didn't know that at the time, and I was truly surprised when the UPI bureau chief hired me.

Some time later both the managing editor and the UPI man told me they knew I had been lying. I would not recommend similar outrageous exaggerations on the part of today's job applicants. If anything, it made my job harder because they had good reason to expect more of me than I was able to produce. The point is, they weren't hiring me for a big job. All they were doing was giving me a chance to get in the door. The rest was up to me. I wasn't fully aware of that, of course. What was most important to me at the time was getting the job, and I thought I had bluffed them. The hard fact is, if I had been unable to do the job—with or without my alleged experience—they would have fired me just as quickly as they had hired me. Had I been candid about my ignorance, I might have received more help in the beginning.

As it was, the first few weeks were a disaster. With the bureau chief away on vacation, the other two UPI staffers

saw the moment as a wonderful time to let the new guy—me
—do most of the routine work. After all, I claimed I knew
what I was doing, didn't I? They spent most of their time in a
nearby tavern. Of course, I couldn't do the job, and about
every hour I would call them with what they considered dumb
questions.

It was frustrating and rather scary in that bureau trying to
do the job myself. But it didn't last long, and somehow I got
through—by working overtime, double time, and studying
when I wasn't working. After a few months of that I quit and
went back to the newspaper and the managing editor I had
met originally.

For the next year he trained me. It is not easy to be trained
on the job. Small news operations rarely can afford the
luxury of a trainee position. You have to pull your weight.
For me that meant doing everything twice. I had to rewrite
and rework almost everything I did. Most managing editors
are not known for their diplomacy or tact. When your work
is bad, they tell you so in the bluntest terms, and this particular managing editor was very blunt. Also, the whole process
was time-consuming and irritating for him. It would have
been much easier for him to take my work and fix it himself
rather than taking the time and effort to tell me how to do it.

My base pay was seventy-five dollars a week. After a year,
when I asked for more money, the publisher pointed out rather
brusquely that he had been *nice enough* to *allow* me to work
a full day of overtime each Saturday. Up to that moment I
had not realized that I had had an option of *not* working
Saturdays. Certainly such an option was never offered.

Shortly thereafter I went to work as a kind of press secretary–researcher–speech-writer and traveling companion to
the governor of Idaho for double my newspaper salary. The
governor hired me at the start of a reelection campaign. It
was great fun. I had a very quick course in practical politics,
but after the governor won reelection and the legislature went

home, things slowed down considerably. It began to get boring.

In the meantime, the managing editor, who had never forgiven me for running off from what he considered pure journalism into the clutches of the politicians, ran into the governor at a cocktail party. A woman who owned one of the two television stations in Boise, Idaho, was also at the party. She needed a news director. After hearing that, the managing editor somehow convinced her that she needed me to run her news department. He also convinced the governor that he did not need me.

The next day I got a phone call from the television station manager. He offered me the job of news director. I had never been in a television newsroom. I did not especially like television news, and I certainly did not know much about it. All I knew was that every time the electronic media crowd showed up at a news conference, they came with what seemed to be a staggering number of cameras, lights, and tape recorders. It looked very technical, and when it comes to technical or mechanical ability, I'm the kind who has a hard time setting an alarm clock.

I did not accept the job at first. Bluffing my way through a typewriter seemed to be one thing, but the technical aspects of broadcasting just looked like too much. The challenge of the job, however, also was appealing, and the station manager made another offer. I accepted. The first thing I did was go out and buy a television set. Any twelve-year-old today with an instamatic camera, a tape recorder, a transistor radio, and access to the family television set knows a good deal more about broadcasting and its technology than I knew then.

It was the same thing all over. Starting from scratch, I learned as much as I could as fast as possible without appearing to be too much of a fool in the eyes of my small staff. I was certainly often the fool. And the staff carried me. But I learned. It took fourteen hours a day, and often, seven days a week.

After a couple of years I became the anchorman because the management fired the anchorman we had. I was terrible. My friends tuned in not for the news but for the amusement of watching me in acute embarrassment stumble through a newscast. But I learned.

After a little more time I won an RCA–NBC fellowship to the Columbia Graduate School of Journalism, which is how I got to New York and started climbing up the ladder all over again, but that is enough of the story to illustrate the point. It's rather easy to declare oneself a journalist, but journalism itself is a no-guarantee business with long hours, big personal risks, little job security, and few prospects for getting rich. Is that something for you? I suppose there is no way of knowing until you try it.

This chapter has emphasized the negative, but I must add that there is really nothing that matches the satisfaction of those occasions when one lives up to the challenge of struggling through difficult circumstances to report a story with freshness and clarity—an important story that the listener understands because you have uncovered it and told it well.

There are those moments when one just barely makes it; tearing into a studio with seconds to spare, and pulling it off. Afterward, coming out, the heart still pounds, but a challenge has been met. There is a sense that you have done the *best* job under the circumstances—perhaps not the best job anyone could do, but the best job *you* could with what you had when the moment arrived.

3

How the
Broadcast Industry Works

There are three major radio *and* television commercial networks in the United States. They are: the American Broadcasting Company (ABC), CBS Inc. (formerly the Columbia Broadcasting System), and the National Broadcasting Company (NBC). There are several other radio networks that operate on regional or national levels (such as the Mutual Broadcasting System). There is also the Public Broadcasting Service (PBS), made up of educational and public supported stations across the country. The PBS is sometimes called the fourth network.

Commercial networks are precisely that—commercial. They are run for profit. According to the U. S. Commerce Department the broadcast industry—all the networks and all the local stations and all the broadcast production centers— employed more than 140,000 people in 1974. The Commerce Department also reported that the broadcast industry would receive in the neighborhood of $7 billion in advertising revenue. That figure is expected to go up between 5 and 10 percent every year until at least 1980.

The founders of the three major commercial networks probably never dreamed the industry they were starting would ever turn into the giant it has become. The networks started as small chains of radio stations. First there was NBC in the mid-1920s, then CBS in 1928. ABC came about in the early 1940s when the Federal Communications Commission ordered NBC to get rid of some of its broadcasting stations because it had too many. There was a fear of concentrating too much broadcasting power into too few hands. At the time, NBC had two networks called the Red and the Blue. ABC was fashioned out of what had been NBC stations in the old Blue network.

As the broadcast industry grew, so did the networks' wealth. With that surplus cash, they began to diversify, to buy properties outside of broadcasting. In time those outside properties began making as much money as broadcasting— and then more. By the early 1970s both CBS and NBC made more than half their corporate income from businesses outside of the networks.

Today the parent corporations of the networks own movie theaters and parking lots. They own record companies and make TV sets, radios, and phonographs. They publish books and manufacture parts for weapons. One network owns Hertz cars. Another runs a chain of toy stores and recently sold the New York Yankees after owning them for eight years.

In short, a network is part of a corporation set up to make money, the same as a ball bearing factory or a chemical plant. Generally, the network corporations have been profitable operations. They are publicly owned, which means you, as a private citizen, can share some of those profits by buying corporation stock, which trades on the New York Stock Exchange. As a stockholder, you would have a right to expect dividends. You would have a right to expect the officers of those corporations to feel obliged to run them in a profitable manner.

However, the broadcast industry differs from the ball bearing factory or the chemical plant because it is regulated not only by the pursuit of profit and the expectations of stockholders but also by the government. Broadcasting is obliged to serve the public interest because it uses the public's air-waves. Very often that obligation means providing news pro-grams, documentaries, and public affairs presentations. There-fore, a commercial network is always trying to do two things at the same time: make money and serve the public interest.

The two interests are not always compatible. It should be no surprise that a network is not principally a news gathering organization. In fact, news operations play a curious role in commercial broadcasting if only because they are not very commercial. Many news programs do not make a large profit (and often lose money) because they cost so much to pro-duce and they do not attract the same huge audiences that entertainment shows enjoy.

The late Edward R. Murrow, a very famous broadcast newsman for CBS, summed up well the curious relationships that exist in broadcasting in a speech he made in 1958:

> One of the basic troubles with radio and tele-vision news is that both instruments have grown up as an incompatible combination of show business, advertising, and news. Each of the three is a rather bizarre and demanding profession. And when you get all three under one roof, the dust never settles.

Networks provide entertainment, sports, news programs, and other material to many local broadcasting stations across the country. The networks are connected to those stations by wires, cables, and microwave equipment like an electronic spider web. Program material may be fed directly to virtually any station in the country as well as overseas via satellite.

Local stations find it an advantage to be connected because the networks provide or *service* them with material that they do not have the resources or know-how to produce. When it comes to entertainment programs, the networks themselves may not produce the material. More often than not they buy their programs from a packager or independent producer and then pass it along the electronic web to the local stations. However, the networks always produce their own nightly news programs.

Affiliates

A station connected with a network is known as an affiliate. Each of the three networks is affiliated with roughly 200 local television stations throughout the country and many more radio affiliates. ABC, for example, has more than 1,400 affiliated radio stations. Sponsors who buy time on network programs want their commercials seen or heard on as many stations as possible. Therefore, it is to a network's advantage to have as many affiliates as is reasonably possible. Also, directly or indirectly, the local affiliates pay the networks for providing them with the programs.

The networks do not own these affiliates. Rather, they have entered into deals with local owners to supply their stations with network programming. Network programs are fed electronically to the various stations on a closed circuit. It's up to the stations to pick up that closed circuit network feed and to put it on the air in their local areas. The local station can either immediately broadcast the network material as it comes in or the station can tape it and put the program on at a different hour or even a different date.

Because they are so closely tied to the day's events, network news shows are almost always put on immediately. That is particularly true of radio news programs. Television news programs are delayed sometimes because of the time change problem. A network news show broadcast from New York at 6:30 P.M. Eastern time arrives in California at 3:30 P.M. In that case, the network centers in the western parts of the country tape the programs and rebroadcast them to the local stations in the area at the appropriate hour.

Local radio and television affiliates do not have to rebroadcast everything that their network feeds. For example, what does an affiliated station do if its network feeds a dreadful situation comedy show every Monday for the 8:00 P.M. time slot? If the local program director decides not enough viewers in his area want to watch that program, he can ignore the network feed. In its place he inserts a locally produced program or a program purchased from an independent producer or "packager" outside the network for that time slot.

O&O's

In addition to the affiliated radio and television stations that the networks do not own, there are local stations known as O&O's. They are stations owned and operated by the networks.

The government allows any one person or company to *own* only five local VHF television stations and up to seven FM and seven AM radio stations. The government sets a limit because it does not want any one person or company to get a monopoly on the communications system in this country. Well-run local stations, particularly television stations, can be big money-makers. Each of the three networks owns its full legal complement of five VHF stations and a number of radio stations. CBS, for example, owns WCBS–TV station in New York. ABC and NBC also have O&O's in New York.

O&O's are in the bigger cities, the major markets. A big city like New York or Chicago or Los Angeles is called, in broadcast terms, a major market because there are a lot of potential buyers there. A little town is a small market. A beginning broadcast journalist or technician often starts out in a small market and then moves up to a major market.

As the term *market* implies, a network is basically just a wholesaler. Networks offer their products to local affiliated stations across the country.

Independents

There are stations in the country that are not affiliated with any network. These are independent stations called indys. An indy can be a very profitable radio or television station. One often finds independent stations in major markets where there are also three network affiliates. In New York, for example, there are six local commercial television stations—the three network affiliates and three independent stations. Indys get their material by buying movies, syndicated programs, network reruns, and by producing their own programs, which, of course, include news.

Summary

Commercial stations in this country, then, fall into one of three categories: the affiliate, the O&O, and the indy. Outside of those three categories there are the educational and public broadcast stations operated on government subsidies, grants, and public donations. Commercial networks are merely parts of large conglomerates, and they are operated for profit. (In 1972, for example, CBS hired a thirty-seven-year-old finance wizard from the International Paper Company to serve as the corporation's new president.)

News operations are not greatly profitable, but they play a major role in broadcasting's obligation to serve the public interest. Networks are best equipped to supply national and international news reports to local affiliates. Their news product, therefore, is valuable. Also, a good news department—whether it is local or network—builds prestige. It is difficult for a station or a network to build an image of responsibility, fairness, and concern for the public good with an endless series of situation comedies, westerns, and murder mysteries. Entertainment shows come and go. A news operation is substantial. It is also very influential in the molding of public opinion.

The Rating Game and News

There is a good deal of bargaining, arm-twisting, and guessing between the affiliates and the networks at the start of every television season when new entertainment shows come out. To a degree, the affiliated stations can pick and choose among the shows offered by their networks. Usually it is left up to the local program director to choose which programs will be picked up and put on the air, which ones will not be carried. That is, in broadcast terms, which programs the director will clear or not clear.

The same pick-and-choose process also applies to network nightly news shows and documentaries. Over the years many affiliates have not cleared even their own network's nightly news show. To a large degree what clears and does not clear depends on a program's rating.

Ratings are the results of carefully selected surveys to determine a program's popularity across the country. Obviously the ratings will have much to do with determining how attractive a particular program will be to a sponsor. A high rating for a show—such as "Bonanza" enjoyed for years—means a lot of people are watching it. Therefore, the broadcaster can charge higher rates to the sponsor who wants to get his commercial into that program.

As I've said, news programs never attract the huge audiences entertainment programs capture, but all local stations are licensed by the government and are under the jurisdiction of the Federal Communications Commission (FCC). Local stations must get their licenses renewed every three years. At renewal time they have to show proof of serving the public interest in terms of public affairs and news programming. For that reason most local affiliates regularly clear their network's major news programs. Lamentably, that is not true of documentaries. Even the best documentaries often suffer from very low clearances because local program directors do not think a large enough percentage of their audience will watch. Instead, they may insert an old movie or something else in that network time slot. Because of low clearances, network public affairs programs often are not scheduled in the traditional prime time hours.

The success of a local television station and its network is often closely related. For example, many, if not most, stations across the country precede the nightly network news program with local news programs. The local news show is the *lead in*. If it is a successful program with high ratings, the network news program that follows is likely to enjoy better ratings in that area because viewers are already tuned to that station. If the lead in is poor, the network rating is likely to be lower than what it could be. The same thing happens at the end of the evening, only in reverse. Most local stations have a 10:00 or 11:00 P.M. local news program following the network's prime time entertainment shows. If the network's last prime time show has a high rating in the area, it is reasonable to expect that the local news program following or *coming out* of the network shows will have better ratings.

Radio affiliates have a somewhat more distant relationship with their networks. Most radio air time is filled locally with disc jockeys, phone-in programs, and the like. Radio affiliates normally pick up the network's hourly national news broadcasts. Also, they may clear sports programs or special events, such as space shots and presidential addresses, offered by the network. Some radio affiliates clear a lot more network material than others. In contrast to radio, however, roughly 60 percent of local television programming comes from the networks. There is not as much demand for network material on local radio because those stations fill their prime time (or drive time) hours with their own talents. There was a time, of course, before television was available, when network entertainment programs were a key to a local radio station's success, but this is no longer true.

Where Do You Fit In?

In the beginning a young broadcast journalist fits in wherever he or she can. It might be a school broadcast station, a small local radio or television station, or even a closed circuit operation. In coming years newcomers increasingly may start with jobs in the highly informal and explorative cable television field. It may be helpful, however, to discuss briefly the two present major job markets for broadcast news personnel: commercial network and local news divisions. What are these places like to work in?

Network News

Network news operations are big, and the very bigness of them can make a low-level job very small, as a private's job in the middle of the whole U. S. Army can be very small. NBC news once advertised that it had a staff of 800 employees. The exact numbers are not important; the general size of each operation is for the individual who may be one of those 800.

The bigness of network operations is both good and bad. For an established professional eager to reach the widest audience, the scope and influence of a network operation is obvious. The immense facilities and technical skills available are obvious. But the drawbacks of working in a large, bureaucratic organization also should be easily imagined.

Additionally, network news operations are built on strong unions. The job one does in the network is almost always hedged in by strictly enforced union regulations. Both the union structure and the advantages and disadvantages of big, bureaucratic organizations in terms of a beginner are discussed more completely in separate chapters. Generally speaking, however, network news people are the indulged step-children of the broadcast industry. They are step-children because the broadcast industry grew up as an entertainment and sales medium—not as a news medium. There is a clear division between the news department and the rest of a network's program departments. The news operation is usually in totally separate buildings, or at least separate office floors and studios. Working network news people do not usually rub shoulders with TV entertainment stars. They are in two different worlds.

Network news operations are generally supervised out of New York and Washington with key bureaus spotted around the country and overseas. The object of a regularly broadcast network news program is to present briefly the major national and international developments of the day or of the hour. Usually, network radio broadcasts a five-minute news summary every hour. That news program is known as an hourly. That operation goes on around the clock. Television's major network output comes in the nightly news programs.

Both radio and television network news programs are fed to local stations in every region and town in the country. It is important to recognize that those affiliated stations are owned and operated by people of every political, moral, and economic belief. A network report, therefore, is delivered as impartially as possible and from the viewpoint of national interest. The national viewpoint, as well as the considerations that go into deciding what an important national story is, can be very different from what a single community in Alabama or Maine considers an important news story.

For example, the outcome of a mayoral election in a small Iowa town can be the most important story of the day in that area. Even a crucial high school football game can be very important to a particular region. But the outcome of the mayor's race or the football game doesn't make much difference to anybody living two thousand miles away. In that sense, then, a network news person generally deals in reports that have only national importance or reflect national trends. In the same way that network news people are somewhat divorced from the overall workings of the network's other program departments, network news people are somewhat divorced from the big stories of individual towns or regions unless they have national significance. A network is not part of any one community. Instead, its news division strives to report what's going on in the whole country and the world.

Local News

A good local radio or television station, commonly known as a local, is part of its community. It reflects a community's goals, shares its triumphs, airs its shortcomings. It is part of the rhythm of the community, unconsciously reflecting its moods and patterns. As part of the area it cannot be separated from the community interests. A bad local station is one satisfied to program hour after hour of syndicated, prepackaged junk and jingles and perhaps five minutes of news ripped off the Associated Press or United Press International news wires. People who work for a good local station are part of the community that they cover in their news programs. That sense of long-range working involvement with a community is not shared by most network news people.

There is also a difference in the style and format of a local station's news show as compared to a network's production, and it is not only a difference in quality. Unfortunately, however, the network's news programs have become the standard of measurement. A good local news operation is called that all too often because it apes the network style. A good local reporter is so called because he does a convincing imitation of David Brinkley. It is unfortunate, because network and local news programs are serving two different interests in two different ways. The difference should involve both style and content.

The basic format of network television news has not

changed much from its beginnings two decades ago. Anchor-men with their own minor peculiarities have come and gone. Graphics and film techniques have improved. The amount of air time given to news has increased. However, the format, itself, has remained, perhaps prematurely hardened into form.

That is less true at the local level. There one finds room for more innovative techniques. Local news shows are often more relaxed. A minute of local time on the air is more read-ily available and less expensive than a minute of network time.

Also, change—new formats, styles, personalities—at the network level comes slowly and is done with caution. Change is directed by human decision makers—men who spent a lot of time doing a thing one way. That one way becomes com-fortable and dependable. Moreover, there are a lot more de-cision makers at the network level—some brave and inno-vative, some not. Change and attempts at doing things new ways is easier to accomplish at the local level.

Comparing a good, innovative local news operation to that of a network, one is reminded of the local hot rod clubs around the country, many of whose members are teenagers with little or no engineering experience. Yet they will take a car, old or new, and literally redesign it: chop, channel, lower it, raise it, strip the chrome, lead it, deck it, reupholster it, soup the engine or build a new one. Essentially those teen-agers are rebuilding and redesigning Detroit's finest, some-times with a final effect more aesthetically pleasing than the original. At the least, those custom cars reflect their young builders' tastes and moods rather than those of some designer in Michigan.

That is not to say the professional Detroit designers are less talented. It is their job to design cars that all kinds of peo-ple will buy. The hot rodders have the freedom to tinker and experiment that the mass producers do not possess.

Local stations have somewhat the same freedom as the hot

rodders. There is nothing to say a news program cannot start with the weather, for example. Network television news does not even report the weather unless there is some compelling reason. A network news program is closely timed and tightly synchronized. A local station may decide to tell the day's events through an informal gathering of reporters simply discussing what they've covered. Such a format may be less efficient in delivering the largest number of news reports in a half-hour segment, but it is only inefficient in the same sense that a hot rod club rebuilding a car is less efficient than a Detroit assembly line.

Moreover, if a local television format is not working as the producers hoped, it can be changed—virtually overnight. Networks do not move that fast. Chances of failure before an audience of millions are not taken lightly. Changes are made, to be sure, but only with great caution. For example, nationwide opinion surveys often are taken before a network anchorman is fired or a new one hired.

In some respects, however, change is coming faster to the networks than many managers realize. Working at the network level today, one senses currents of change running through the entire industry.

As the country becomes more literate and as tastes become more sophisticated, demands and interests of the viewer become far more specialized and fragmented. One kind of news format, one kind of personality on the air, will do no longer.

Again, think of the automobile industry. Cars are still mass produced. But a buyer willing to wait for a car that he puts on order has today almost an infinite variety of options. By computer count, a buyer of a single family car now has millions of options if he considers all the possibilities of color, interior, transmission, tires, engines, radio, and so on.

Obviously, broadcasting—at least in television and radio news—has not reached that level of diversity. But with the growth of cable television and satellites and closed circuit sound and sight systems, not to mention the potential of video cassettes, great change is on the horizon. It may very well be that the newcomer to electronic news will find his or her start or lifelong career in those areas.

4

Education and
Early Experience

Broadcast news involves the talents of many people. Print journalists, newspaper and magazine reporters, that is, often joke about broadcasting's "group journalism." It *is* a group process. A lot of broadcast reporters don't like that because they are forced to depend on many others to get their stories on the air, but that's the way it is.

People involved in the broadcast news business are divided, roughly, into two categories: editorial workers and technicians. That is not a wholly accurate division, but, again, that's the way it's done.

Editorial workers are the writers, editors, reporters, producers, and directors. At the network level editorial workers don't operate any equipment outside their mini-sized, portable tape recorders because of union restrictions. They don't shoot film, they don't edit tape, they don't load the projectors. They cannot operate any machines connected with electronic journalism. They are not even supposed to move a chair on a television news set. (That's a property man's job.) In theory, editorial workers don't do anything but give directions, write, produce, and deliver on the air. The rest is up to the technicians.

That is not how it works at small or even medium sized

local stations where union restrictions are not rigid or don't exist.

The problem with the word *technician* is that it's rather limited, at least in the sense that Americans use the word. The performance of the technician is as crucial to the success of a broadcast news report as the performance of any editorial personnel. It is shallow to describe a creative camera person as a technician in our usual mechanistic sense of that word. It is unfair to term a talented film editor merely as a technician. Some camera people and film and radio tape editors are creative geniuses. *Craftsmen and artisans* would be more accurate for describing many of the technicians in broadcasting, but because *technician* is the word used, let it stand—in the broadcast industry's sense of the word.

The education of the editorial worker is primarily academic, combined with as much practical experience as is possible or reasonable. The education of the technician is almost always a combination of book learning and advanced technical training or apprenticeship to gain the necessary electronic, photographic, or editing experience. Let's first discuss the education of the editorial worker.

Education

For years journalism leaned heavily on the notion of the natural newsman, the fellow who came up through the school of hard knocks, who had a nose for news—and other such clichés. (I use the term *newsman* intentionally. For years women were never taken seriously as bona fide hard news reporters. There were exceptions, of course, but not many.)

A colleague of mine writing a book on political reporters came upon a very revealing article by Leo C. Rosten in the June, 1937, issue of *Journalism Quarterly*. In a survey of the 127 main Washington correspondents (that is, a large number of the most important journalists in the country) only half of them had finished college. Eight did not have high school diplomas, and two had no high school education at all! All that began to change after World War II, but the change did not come automatically, and the new breed of college educated journalists who arrived in the early 1950s were not altogether welcome.

As the country and journalism became more sophisticated, more troubled, and vastly more complex, one could feel among the old-timers in the newsroom a longing for the "old days." As a young man in journalism I can remember the nostalgic stories told by veteran reporters about long gone colleagues. Everything seemed to them much simpler "back then."

The truth is, yesterday's newsman often came from what was really an apprenticeship program. In those days a young fellow could start as a copy boy and work himself up to becoming a reporter. He could do that without much more than a high school diploma and techniques learned from the seasoned reporters in the newsroom.

There was also an air of swashbuckling mystery surrounding the profession of journalism. In the movies the foreign correspondent always wore a trench coat and came up with a big scoop that solved something at one blow. There are still big scoops in journalism (although one does not hear the word used seriously in newsrooms today), but a big scoop in 1971 was the breaking of the Pentagon Papers; a story that took tens of thousands of words to tell and may have required a college history major to understand.

The big scoop of 1972 and 1973 was the Watergate Affair. That was a story broken by two young men scarcely thirty, one of whom looked like a hippie to the more polished Washington veteran reporters. Moreover, the way they went charging around to get their stories would have disgraced any Hollywood version of yesterday's suave correspondent. And, finally, nothing about Watergate came out pure and simple.

The scandal dribbled out in bits and pieces. It required extraordinary perseverance and the intellectual process necessary to distill all the bits and pieces and to put them into an overall picture. The two reporters who led the way in the Watergate Affair were called the kids.

There always has been a kind of anti-intellectual bias in the country's newsrooms—a suspicion of the college kid who "doesn't know nothing" about real life. To a degree that bias remains, but it is the college kid who has been getting the jobs.

Few major journalistic institutions today are hiring beginning reporters, producers, even copy boys (or desk assistants, as they are called in broadcasting) unless they have at least some college training. The reason is simple: All things being equal, the beginner with more education has the advantage— he or she knows more. The employers figure they are getting more for their money. Journalism, like medicine, is increasingly turning to the specialist: the science reporter, the labor reporter, the civil rights reporter, the urban affairs reporter, the economic reporter, the political reporter.

It comes down to this simple rule for the person interested in a journalism career: the more formal education, the better. But what kind of education? Here are my personal observations and recommendations:

- High school is not enough;
- A college major in journalism alone probably is unwise;
- Graduate school study in journalism is worthwhile but generally most useful if delayed until after a few years of practical, on-the-job experience;
- Schools for announcers are to be generally avoided;
- Learn to type and to write on a typewriter. Even ninth grade is not too soon. You cannot be a journalist unless you can type.

The importance of college is not the degree (although it will help in getting a job at the start) but the training it provides in acquiring the basic skills and experience of learning quickly and dealing with a wide variety of ideas and intellectual challenges. If nothing else, college helps to teach a young person to absorb and to organize information. That is a lot of what journalism is all about.

Why not a college major in journalism? For years the Columbia Graduate School of Journalism has had an excellent admissions policy: no undergraduate journalism majors are accepted unless they have had at least 96 credit hours in other liberal arts fields. Usually that refers to an applicant who is a liberal arts major with some journalism courses and some on-the-job experience or someone who took a double major in college—journalism and something else.

Why? A good many journalism courses are, basically, a study of the nuts and bolts of the profession: how to write a headline, edit copy, do lay-out, edit film or tape, experiment with closed circuit studio work, and so on. All of it is good experience with the mechanics of journalism, but it is not very intellectually stimulating. One often hears old-timers in the newsroom claim they can teach a bright novice more in ninety days on the job than he or she can learn in four years of college journalism.

In the sense that the old-timers make that boast, they are probably right. There are some basic formulas to reporting, especially hack reporting. There are a few basic formats that will serve the mediocre reporter in covering the usual routine of fires, murders, elections, and so on. The object of the true professional is to avoid falling into those tired formulas. There will always be murders and elections and fires. They will require reporting, but they do not have to be endlessly reported in the same way, with only the names, dates, or figures changed. New forms and fresh styles are needed.

Am I suggesting one ignore journalism in college or high

school? No. I am suggesting major study in other areas. For the future journalist I would recommend history, political science, English, the social sciences, or a combination of virtually any fields one finds interesting. At the same time I would recommend as much journalism as one can find time for; certainly basic introductory courses combined with work on campus publications, broadcasts, part-time work at local stations, or whatever is available.

My point is this: If I had to make a choice between a course on copy editing and, say, an introduction to oriental philosophy, I'd choose the philosophy. As a working journalist I edit every day and probably will do so for the rest of my career. I've never taken a course in oriental philosophy.

An experienced and well-read reporter always startles a beginner with how much he or she adds or subtracts from the immediate facts of the story at hand. It is the background or the cultural setting to the facts that often makes important an otherwise meaningless story.

Why do I think graduate journalism schools are worthwhile but suggest working for a few years in the real world of journalism before going to one? Let me qualify the recommendation by saying graduate school is worthwhile if it is more than a glorified trade school. By nature most journalists are pragmatists, less interested in theory than practice. Journalism students do not want to hear about it—they want to do it. They are interested in jobs. They want the skills that will put them out on the street in a year or two with a good job.

That pressure is understandable and, for any school, dangerous. Certainly a balance has to be struck between the theoretical and the practical. The danger is for the school to degenerate into little more than a series of copy editing courses and lessons on how to write professionally rather than how to think, to analyze, and to structure. The thought process is harder to teach than the mechanics.

Most of us working in the field rarely have much time for

reflection on what journalism is really about. We are not generally columnists or commentators. A story has to be reported and we do it—usually as fast as possible. We do it with the skills gained from past experience. We do it with what talents we have. We do it with whatever intellectual background we have to bring to the report. It becomes instinctual. But are we doing it the best way? Should we consider another approach? Is the way that we are reporting the story really meaningful?

Unfortunately, a working journalist does not have much time for that kind of musing. Whether something is done well or poorly is often rated in terms of the immediate circumstances: Did it get done on time? Do the facts add up? When one is in the middle of the deadline battle, it's hard to tell. Therefore, one of the most useful aspects about graduate school is the tutorial time available to study better ways to do things, away from the pressure of the immediate deadline, where there is time to consider new ways to approach old problems, time to consider new problems. I do not mean to limit the approach purely to philosophical considerations. Also, graduate schools can be good places for the broadcaster to learn new methods for solving old technical problems.

I suggest working for a while before going on to graduate school because it is important to know what one doesn't know; to know the area one is weak in, to know what questions to ask a professor or a professional, to know what one might like to explore further. A graduate school can provide a kind of touchstone for judgment and a measure for one's own work; that is, it provides a more educated sense of what is good and bad, and why.

That brief outline of recommendations is purely personal. In its most simple form I am suggesting that the potential journalist take an academic program in high school, major in a liberal arts discipline (or science, for that matter) in college, and take journalism as a second major or a minor. At the end of this book there is a list of organizations that keep track of colleges and universities offering courses of one kind or another in journalism.

I should note here that many employers and news directors would not agree with my recommendations on education. When a news director has a job opening, he wants to hire someone who can step in and do the job immediately. Nobody wants to train someone if he doesn't have to, although the fact is, there is almost always some on-the-job training necessary for any new employee. But young people have to be aware that the immediate demands of the job market and the process of preparing themselves for high caliber, long-range careers in journalism are not the same things. There are usually too few years available for higher education. Then the realities catch up and a person has to make a living. Once that process starts, there is little time for going back to college.

Schooling for the Technician

For the young person interested in becoming a news camera person, a film editor, a sound technician, a lighting expert, an engineer, and so on, a basic high school education is essential. Beyond that, there are excellent technical schools available. In fact, the schooling available for technicians is generally more specific and job-oriented than that available to the editorial worker.

The line between the technician and the editorial worker has become most blurred in the field of photography. Many of today's younger camera people are college graduates. (Women are slowly getting into the field of professional newsreel film work. For that reason the single word *cameraman* is no longer accurate. But the broadcast industry has not yet invented a single word to include both men and women.) For many of them cinematography began as a hobby and became a vocation. They found that they would rather make films than anything else. From that point it becomes a question of economics. Television news stations are sources of employment.

Newsreel production is often very different from artistic movies or features, but the basic skills are the same. Moreover, many documentaries receive as much loving care and artistic effort as a feature movie. There is, however, the dimension of reality in news work. News events are not staged or directed by news personnel.

There are a number of good schools that provide training in advanced techniques of cinematography. A report from the American Film Institute showed that by 1972 there were film and television courses offered at 613 colleges. Out of that number, 51 of them offered degrees in film. Those figures are astounding when one considers virtually no similar courses were even offered ten years earlier.

It is impossible to recommend any one school or even a number of them, because film schools are very much like art schools. Each has a different style and emphasis. Some lean heavily on practical exercise. Some rely more on theory and analysis. The amount and quality of each school's technical facilities vary greatly, depending on its budget and purpose. Some schools admit students without formal higher education or university affiliation.

It's up to the camera person who wants to take advanced courses to find out specifically what he or she is looking for. One must talk to other camera people in the industry. One can consult the college catalog available in most libraries. The best course of action would be to visit a number of film schools. Tips and ideas on career employment abound at film school centers.

A formal film course is not necessary for a successful career in news work. Certainly such course work is no guarantee to employment. But the course is usually fun. The experience can do no harm, and it might open doors that otherwise would be hard to find or open.

At the television news level many camera people are trained through the apprenticeship method. Any beginner is urged to visit local stations and to ask questions.

A newcomer usually starts at a small station and works up into bigger markets according to his or her ability to shoot news film that tells the story. Experience is mandatory for upward movement. In the big cities camera people are required to be members of a powerful union. It can be extremely difficult for the newcomer to join. (Broadcast unions will be discussed more fully later.)

There are two kinds of educational directions open to the broadcast engineer. One is the university program leading to a degree in electrical engineering. The other involves a wide variety of nonuniversity electronics courses offered throughout the country.

Almost all of the technicians working with the machines and electronic apparatus in broadcasting are known as engineers. This broad use of the term has to do with unions and the fact that the employees like the title. Conceivably, the person who sweeps the floor in the video tape room could be called the floor maintenance engineer. The point is that the word *engineer* is used very loosely in the industry.

There are, of course, the traditional electrical engineers with advanced college degrees in the field of electronic communications. If a person is fascinated by the electronics of broadcasting and has the time, money, and ability to get a college degree, that is unquestionably the best course.

Engineering got a great boost with the space age and military contracts. When work in aerodynamics slowed down, a great many engineers were out of work. Curiously enough, few of them made it into broadcast engineering. Perhaps their training was too specialized for easy adaptation to another field.

The greatest demand today for noncollege engineers in broadcasting is in the maintenance and development fields. As the machines become more automated and simple to run, they get more complicated on the inside. It is the maintenance engineer, not the operator, who is most likely to succeed. Because of that, the increasing demand in broadcasting is for men and women who know how to fix the machines as well as how to operate them.

An engineer with a college degree in electronics most likely will end up in the management side of a broadcast operation. The electrical engineer in broadcasting, for example, may be in charge of planning and installation of new technology. For the noncollege engineer, a number of advanced courses are available.

Some require no more than two years of high school to get into. Most of the advanced programs require at least a high school proficiency in the basics of algebra and some higher mathematics. Schools that offer electronics courses sometimes offer basic or refresher math courses. Whatever the course, broadcast engineers are not trained specifically for news production. They are trained in engineering, which is used in news.

The broadcast engineer or technician may be the one who puts together a news report or an entire news program on video tape under the direction of a producer or a news director. He or she may be the video tape editor, radio's audio tape editor, the recording specialist, the electronic cameraman, the technical director, or the maintenance engineer who keeps the machines running. Video tape production is a major part of broadcasting today, and it will become even more important as the years go on. It is rapidly becoming a specialty of its own within the field of engineering.

At the networks, engineers usually are assigned to the kind of work that best fits their experience, ability, and preference. Engineers have a tendency to become connected with certain kinds of productions—whether it's sports, or news, or entertainment programs—and to stay there. Local stations with smaller staffs do not have that luxury and the broadcast engineer works wherever he is needed.

Most technicians working in news today in photography, sound recording, lighting, and technical direction learned their skills through formal or informal apprenticeship programs. They started as someone's helper and went on from that point—depending on their ability, interest, and advanced training. Television grew up too fast to allow development of proper training programs at the time they were needed. Much of broadcasting's technology was invented as the industry moved along. For that matter, much is still being invented rather informally. There isn't a station or a network in the country that doesn't have some strange piece of equipment somewhere that an engineer built just to meet an immediate need or because there was nothing on the market to fill a particular demand.

For studio and control room jobs outside of engineering there are few advanced programs available. But there are many introductory courses. A growing number of colleges are developing broadcast programs where students learn to direct and produce their own closed circuit campus productions. The worth of such programs depends on the background of the instructors and the professional quality of the facilities provided.

Lighting is a science in itself. It is the basis of all photography. Usually lighting courses are part of graphic arts programs. Universities in California long affiliated with the motion picture industry are best known for their graphic arts programs as applied to film and tape productions.

The techniques and science of sound recording are not widely taught. At best the basics are presented and the recording technician takes it from there. Sound recording is thoroughly discussed in books and written texts provided by major manufacturers of audio tape and recording equipment. Much can be learned by home study and personal initiative. With the development of home stereo, the science of recording has become a major American hobby and is becoming increasingly demanding because of cultural tastes. The most sophisticated recording sessions I have ever seen and heard were done by rock groups who are years ahead of recording techniques now employed in broadcast news.

Some stations and networks are sending employees back to school for advanced training necessary to keep up with the new technology in many fields. The advantage for the young person today is obvious: He or she can start advanced education where the older professional may have left off.

There are a number of electronics institutes throughout the country. These courses concentrate on the basics of machinery and equipment. Some specialize in areas such as sound recording and amplification. Others offer good introductory courses to video tape operations and electronic cameras. It is likely that such a school is relatively near anyone interested in pursuing an electronics career.

Courses in specific areas of broadcast production are sometimes offered by major manufacturers who, of course, want technicians to be familiar with their equipment. Such courses can be expensive but may be worthwhile for particular kinds of instruction.

Some state colleges are developing broadcast programs with facilities far more elegant though not as technical as those provided by specialized, private institutions.

Electronic journalism, a field opening up to women now, cannot function without engineers and technicians. There is always a job opening somewhere for the trained individual. Young people with up-to-date schooling have an educational advantage, but they do not have experience. The best any school can do is simulate real conditions. No school can duplicate the demands made by the real world of broadcasting. That is the veteran's advantage. The veteran has performed under pressure. In short, the veteran has experience.

Early Experience

There is no compelling reason for the high school senior who wants to be a lawyer or a doctor to start hanging around a hospital or a courtroom, although one's interest may take one there. For the future broadcast journalist or engineer there are several reasons to start looking into part-time or summer jobs in local stations as soon as possible.

Early job exposure in a radio or television station—no matter how menial the job—often is what gives direction to a future career. There are many different kinds of professions under the single umbrella of broadcast journalism. It is valuable to work even as a messenger or as a copy boy to discover what best fits one's talents and interests. It may be news writing. It may be photography. It may be engineering. It may be on-air reporting. This book describes the many jobs connected with broadcast news, but it can never take the place of seeing for oneself what goes on in a broadcast operation.

Another reason for an early start is that broadcasting is so much of a young person's game. The industry's emphasis is on youth. But perhaps the best reason for early experience is the fact that on any level the industry's standard of measure is *performance*.

Social connections, job connections—even good manners —are secondary to performance; that is, the ability to do the job under pressure. In the course of turning out a news report for broadcast, something almost always goes wrong. An interview falls through or is no good, the film gets lost, the tape recorder breaks, the director misses a cue, but the broadcast must go on at the scheduled time.

Performing under pressure means the ability to do the job under conditions that suggest it cannot—or will not—be done as planned. When the moment arrives for the news broadcast, either the report is there on the air or it isn't. There is no "stop the presses."

Theory and education aside, then, a crucial element of performance is experience in dealing with the unexpected. The earlier one begins, the sooner one gets it.

The only way to learn the language of broadcast journalism, that curious combination of technology and content, is to work in the field. Because reporters and producers rely on a variety of machines to record or amplify their material for broadcasting, a somewhat standardized set of techniques and terminology has emerged. Actually *terminology* is an unnecessarily fancy word; *jargon* is more like it—a kind of shorthand vocabulary that editorial people and technical people use to communicate with one another.

Like all jargon talkers, broadcasters seem to relish the mystery that surrounds their operations. The truth is none of it is much more difficult to master than the jargon of football or cookbook recipes, but it takes time.

The jargon usually refers to a kind of machine or a process (*VTR* for video tape recorder; *double system* for shooting film and recording sound separately; and so on). The jargon can be explained in a classroom or a textbook, but like a foreign language it is difficult to learn unless you are actually using it. The earlier one gets to feeling comfortable in the real world of broadcasting and its tools, the better.

What must happen is that the technology (and the jargon for it) become subordinate to the content. The principal concern of the journalist cannot be the technical elements that go into doing a broadcast report. The principal concern must be the story itself; that is, content. To get that content across, the journalist must be able to use or to understand the technical facilities of broadcasting reflexively, as a typist uses a typewriter. The typewriter is merely a tool used to write something. What is important to the writer is the content of the material, not the construction of the typewriter.

Doing even a menial job helps the beginner learn what the business is all about. It provides an opportunity to watch other people doing a job and to decide if that's something one *really* wants to do for a living. It may convince the person that it is not the career for him or her. Either way, the sooner one knows, the better.

5

What Are the Jobs?

In a large broadcast news operation there are many separate and specific job categories, each with its own union boundaries and prerogatives, which are jealously guarded. And, as always in broadcasting, there is a necessary marriage between the functions of the editorial workers and the technicians.

In small local newsrooms many of the jobs are done by one person. The news director may also be the assignment editor, reporter, and anchor person. He may serve as a cameraman as well. All of the staff may double as film or audio tape editors and even help out with the film developing. Such job combinations are good sources of experience. Because the jobs tend to overlap in small operations, it is hard to separate them; but in large organizations, here is how they break down.

On the editorial side, there are four broad career job categories:

- Writer
- Assignment editor
- Correspondent (reporter)
- Producer

Above these categories are news directors, news managers, vice presidents and presidents of news.

News is gathered and put together in the field—that is, out on location where the story occurs—in the newsroom, and in the studio. The technicians working with the editorial staff are:

In the Field (one or more)

- Camera person
- Sound person
- Light person (electrician)
- Engineer (for live production or radio)

For documentary production there also may be:

- Assistant camera person
- Grip (property person)
- Gaffer (chief electrician)
- Director
- Unit manager (handles business arrangements, accommodations, finances)

In the Studio (one or more)

- Director
- Associate director (AD)
- Technical director (TD)
- Audio control
- Video control
- Engineers
- Stage manager (floor director)
- Studio camera
- Lighting director
- Electrician
- Property person
- Carpenter
- Grip

- Make up
- Teleprompter operator

In the Newsroom (one or more)

- Video tape editor, operator
- Film editor
- Audio tape editor
- Graphic artist
- Projectionist
- Researcher
- Unit manager
- Desk assistant
- Secretary
- Production assistant
- Traffic (handles arrangements for electronic feed lines)
- Transport (handles shipping and receiving of news material)
- Courier
- Teleprompter typist
- Lab technician

Couriers generally use motorcycles to race about picking up and delivering film and radio material from field locations and airports. They work under the direction of the transport desk. There is a ceaseless flow of material coming in and going out of a newsroom. Unit managers keep track of expenses and budgets. They work directly with the business affairs office of a news operation. The teleprompter typist copies all news copy on a special typewriter that prints in big, bold letters nearly an inch tall. The teleprompter roll is attached to a machine on the studio cameras so that the anchor person can look straight at the camera and read news stories without looking down. An operator controls the machine so that the copy rolls by as it is read.

Some of the jobs listed are not performed right in the newsroom or the studio. The video tape operation or projection or film processing may be done elsewhere because that is how the building is laid out. Ideally, however, all of the functions and jobs listed for each heading would be done in one area.

Supporting all of these jobs are sundry assistants, trainees, and others whose titles and functions fall somewhere in between. Walking into a newsroom just before air time, one sees a number of people dashing about. Each person has a job. The object is to coordinate all of them so that when the news program goes on the air, each part meshes into a single, coherent whole.

Apart from the daily news operation, there are special events units at each of the networks. Much of that work involves live news productions. They operate with skeleton staffs, swelling in numbers as an event—such as a space shot or an election—approaches. Also, there are documentary units that operate apart from the daily news programs and the special events unit. There is, however, some personnel movement between all of these units.

Finally, in every big operation there are always special job categories created for one person with a unique talent or function. Usually those special categories disappear when the person does.

Big stations and networks necessarily divide job functions along union lines while small operations do not. Because the various jobs are more clearly defined at the network level, I have chosen to describe job categories as they exist at the networks. Bear in mind that at most stations someone has to perform these various tasks no matter what the title. Somebody has to make the decisions. Somebody has to record the sound or shoot the film. Somebody has to process it. Somebody has to edit it. Somebody has to read the copy on the air. Somebody has to direct the program, and somebody has to run the machines. In a small station there may be only three or four "somebodies" to do all these jobs. The more one knows about all of the jobs, the better one can function at any level. Most of that kind of wide-ranging practical experience comes only at the small local station level.

It is possible but not particularly recommended to start at a network. For the beginner, the pay will be low, the job not the most challenging, and it will take rather a long time to move up.

BEGINNERS' JOBS

Desk Assistant

There are almost always job openings at the networks for desk assistants, which is a fancy title for copy boys. The job pays miserably. In 1973 a desk assistant in New York started at $96 a week, although there is usually a lot of overtime work available. The turnover and absentee rate is predictably high. After six months they made $99; after a year, $106; after a year and a half, $108; and after two years, $116.

Many desk assistants are college students either going to school part time or on leave of absence. Most come with some vague notion of getting into the broadcast news business and use the job as an opportunity to look around from the inside. Occasionally one runs into a female desk assistant, but most are young men. There is no particular reason for this, and the networks will hire women as well as men for the job. In fact, they are beginning to urge female potential journalists to start there.

The desk assistant's job is principally clerical. A desk assistant, or DA, is also known as a gofer, since he's often asked to go for something—coffee, cigarettes, messages, or whatever.

DA's spend most of their time stripping stories off the news wire machines (AP, UPI, Reuters, and others) and delivering that copy, which comes off in long narrow sheets, to various editorial people around the newsroom. They also answer the phones, place calls, and help to assemble the news show by checking page numbers of scripts, carrying last-minute additions and deletions to the anchor desk, and standing by to do whatever nobody else has the time or the inclination to do.

In terms of career, there is a certain danger in being a DA. The DA is usually in the middle of the daily excitement of a news operation—he or she is part of it—but is *not* functioning as a journalist. The job is simple, the mental demands can be few, and, for some, it becomes too easy to stay with instead of seeking greater challenge elsewhere.

The people who profit most from such a job are those who stay only long enough to become thoroughly familiar with the news operation and then move on. Many young DA's have used the position to trade themselves into more responsible positions in local stations. One young man I know, a college graduate, wrote to 140 stations across the country while working at a network as a DA. His major professional experience was working as a DA, but three stations were impressed enough to offer him a job, among them a reporter-writer position at a rather good but small station in the south. That same young man is now the news director of the local station. It took him two years to rise to that position. Someday he may return to the network, but certainly not as a DA.

One can remain at the network and wait out a promotion. For a particularly bright or at least tenacious young person, it will come. The next step up is usually to the position of production assistant.

Newsroom Secretary

It is helpful to differentiate between the newsroom secretary and other kinds of secretaries. The traditional concept of a secretary is a woman who takes stenography, types, answers the phone, and does various clerical chores. Many newsroom secretaries cannot and are not expected to take dictation. Frequently they function more as assistants than as traditional secretaries. Many are college graduates. None want to remain secretaries.

Like DA's, they take the job to get in the door. They are ambitious for careers in broadcasting and usually make their ambitions known at the outset. Many quit in frustration. The turnover is high because advancement can be slow. At the network level in 1973 they started at about $115 a week. It is usually up to them to prove that they are worth more and can do more.

Officially there is no such thing as a newsroom secretary in any network's personnel roster. Informally, however, everyone recognizes the difference between the career secretary and the secretary looking for a journalism career.

Generalities are dangerous, but the career secretary is often not a college graduate. She is often older, married, perhaps raising a family, and satisfied working regular hours. The top career secretary is the professional executive secretary. Often she works more as an administrative assistant with typists working for her. She is very good at the usual secretarial tasks, as well as dealing with people and pressure. Some such secretaries in the industry make better than $400 a week— and the ones I have seen in action are probably worth more. But that is not the newsroom secretary, who is not interested in secretarial or administrative work no matter how well paid. She wants to move into journalism, and for her, the competition is fierce.

Every time an opening develops above the secretarial level, word moves around very fast, and the women in the newsroom struggle for promotion. Because of the availability of generally well-educated female talent, promotions usually come from within. Traditionally the next step up is to the position of production assistant, assistant to the producer, or researcher. Almost all of the women presently in positions of production or administrative authority in broadcasting began as secretaries of one kind or another. That is no longer necessarily true, and the trend is increasingly away from that slow, tedious route. (See Chapter 9, "Chances for Women and Minority Group Members.") Many young women progressing in news careers today say that whatever the stigma and drudgery attached to secretarial work, without that start they would never be where they are now. A recent survey indicated that 66 percent of the executive women at CBS began in clerical or secretarial roles. But times are changing rapidly, and other women within the industry advise young women to stay away from secretarial work, no matter what the circumstances.

One such woman is Mary Jean Parson, an associate director for planning at ABC who never worked as a secretary. Ms. Parson began her career in off-Broadway theater management. In a survey article on women's positions in broadcasting, she was quoted:

> I would advise a girl starting in the broadcast business to starve or take to the streets before accepting a secretarial job if she wants to get ahead. Once you get into that position it's almost impossible to get out. To say you can start as a secretary and move on up to the top is just not so.

She was speaking more of the standard nine-to-five secretarial position than of the newsroom secretary, but she is not alone in her opinion. There is always a gamble involved. Openings may be slow to develop. A woman may be passed over.

On the other hand, a woman such as NBC's Barbara Walters says she feels a woman should take any position "to get her feet in the door." She started as a secretarial girl Friday in a small New York advertising agency and went to WNBC–TV in New York as a publicist before becoming an associate producer and finally a hostess on the "Today" show.

There is no hard advice one can give a young woman debating the advantages and disadvantages of starting as a secretary in broadcasting. A lot of it depends on the employer: his past record for promoting women out of that position, his promises, or lack of promises. No matter how one appraises the long-run opportunities, however, the beginner has to get in the door somewhere, and sometimes the only way is through a menial job. Incidentally, the same gamble holds true for beginning young men who traditionally have taken desk assistant jobs.

Production Assistants

Production assistants, or PA's, serve as assistants to producers working on particular programs. Those programs can be daily news shows, special events, or documentaries. Their jobs are more interesting and challenging than those of the DA or the newsroom secretary. Much of their time is spent on the technical aspects of radio and television production. There is absolutely no rule of thumb to say how long it takes to move from the job of DA or secretary to PA. Given luck, ability, and sympathetic management, two years probably would be a fair average. A PA has a better job but doesn't make much more money than a DA. In 1971 a network PA started at $95 a week. Some are able to bargain for more money. (Everything in broadcasting is negotiable; the figures given are minimums.)

Outside of the pay, there is much more to be said for a PA's job. Talented PA's rarely stay long in that category because they have a greater chance to show their talents. Moreover, their responsibilities usually exceed their titles. Many PA's are hired at the network level after gaining some production experience at the local station level. The network may put them in the PA position for a while to see what they can do.

For reasons that have to do with the strange ways of broadcast unions (something explained much more fully in the chapter on unions), PA's at ABC and CBS are members of the Directors Guild of America (DGA). PA's at NBC work under different titles and are members of the National Association of Broadcast Employees and Technicians (NABET).

At CBS, PA's frequently proceed from production assistants to associate directors, to director's positions. At ABC they tend to move toward becoming assistant producers, associate producers, and up to full producers. There is certainly no rule governing their career advancement. They might not go anywhere or they might become administrators. I mention only vaguely recognizable trends at those two networks. In 1973 a PA in the Directors Guild and at the top of the pay scale was earning $166 a week.

Researcher

Traditionally, researchers are almost always women. Very frequently they come from the newsroom secretarial ranks. Principally, a researcher's job is to check accuracy, dig up facts, and comb published material (newspapers, magazines, etc.) for news stories. She works in close contact with the editorial staff and generally does not do secretarial work. Researchers invariably create their own jobs. Some are content to sit back and wait until somebody asks them to check a fact or to look up something. Others work on their own and supply producers with constant suggestions. It can be a good position from which to gain recognition. A researcher starts roughly at $160 a week. It is a nonunion job, however, and subject to negotiation. Outstanding researchers have been known to get $450 a week, but not often.

There are always more researchers than jobs available.

Over the years it's been customary for magazines such as *Time, Newsweek,* the women's magazines, other publications, and publishing houses to hire graduates of the prestigious eastern women's colleges as researchers or editorial assistants. The jobs never pay what they are worth, but women eager to put their college educations to work always have provided a ready pool of cheap talent. In broadcasting, as well as publishing, researchers never had much leverage for increased pay or promotion because there have always been so many others willing to take the job. Supply outruns demand.

I have included the job of researcher under the heading of beginner's job, but some women choose it as a career position. Above the rank of researcher the competition becomes even more brisk, the positions less secure, and the demands on a person's time far more exaggerated. For some, the advancement is not worth it.

Unit Manager

Like the job of researcher, the unit manager's position is not necessarily a beginner's job. Unit managers keep track of a program's expenses. They watch over the budget, check expense accounts, and so on. There are unit managers throughout broadcasting. It is not a job limited to news production.

Often a unit manager will accompany a news operation out into the field. There are several unit managers involved in major productions. Unit managers are generally men with business education backgrounds and they usually report to the business affairs office rather than to the news producers. Their positions can be more critical than any of the other jobs listed so far because they often take responsibility for making all necessary business and financial arrangements connected with a production.

Nonetheless, few unit managers remain in that position indefinitely. Invariably they move up into broader administrative positions in the business end of the news production, or they become editorial employees—usually producers. As unit managers they have ample opportunity to observe the workings of a news operation.

Assistant to the Producer

Assistant to the producer is a rather nebulous title that does not mean assistant producer. Some news operations do not have such positions. The duties fall somewhere between those of a producer and a production assistant. An assistant to the producer is actually a person judged not yet ready for the responsibilities of a full producer but above those jobs below. Assistants are paid in the neighborhood of $200 a week.

Assistants to the producer not only conceive news stories but also help to see them through to completion in the newsroom. Sometimes they go out in the field with news crews and correspondents to help gather the material. Also, a good deal of the assistant's time is spent in the newsroom helping to edit stories sent in by correspondents and producers from around the world.

An assistant to the producer is in a good position to move up either to the rank of producer or to the job of a correspondent, depending upon talent and desire.

I must add two last notes about beginners' jobs.

Many who profited most from starting at the bottom were those who came, looked around, and discovered that broadcast journalism was not for them. In the course of that discovery they may have found related fields that were more to their liking.

Others came and decided not to leave for smaller operations offering more immediate responsibility. No matter how difficult the ladder looks, there is always room for the bright and truly imaginative beginner. There is a premium on originality in broadcasting. There is a premium on talent. There is also a premium on the individual who has the persistence to get his or her talent and originality recognized. That persistence is simply part of the industry's natural selection process.

It is that process that so often dismays and discourages newcomers. They may feel they have ample talent and brilliant ideas (particularly in comparison to the people who have the jobs they want), but nobody seems to care or recognize them. Some broadcast operations can become so entrenched that they do not have room for the bright beginner. They become more like civil service bureaus than creative imaginative broadcast operations. Those are operations from which to flee—but not until the newcomer has given them a fair trial. And, though it may sound rather brutal or cynical, it is a fact that the person who waits patiently, depending on a promotion purely through fairness and the employer's recognition of talent, is likely to wait a good long time. It is up to the individual to prove his or her abilities—over and over again. If the abilities are really there, sooner or later they will be recognized.

CAREER JOBS

Writer

An irony of broadcast news today is that the writer is becoming obsolete. Writing, itself, is not. It's more a question of who is doing the writing.

Broadcasting grew up as an entertainment and sales medium. There was a time when not many in broadcasting knew much about news. Instead of journalists, the broadcasting industry had announcers—men with fine voices and no training in journalism. As news programs rapidly became more important, it was apparent that it would be easier to hire news writers to write what the golden throats could read than to teach these readers to write. It was then that news writers became very important. They came from newspapers and magazines. They knew a lot about news but not much about broadcasting or film or tape.

A few of the younger announcers made the switch and became true journalists, but not many. Most were, and are, making too much money as staff announcers—doing commercials, announcing station breaks, perhaps hosting live programs, and sometimes doubling as disc jockeys. Because of the union fee schedule, which determines the amount of money to be paid each time a person's voice, name, or face is used, many staff announcers make enormous sums. A few make in the neighborhood of a quarter of a million dollars a year just doing commercials and announcing.

In seriously news oriented stations today, mere readers or staff announcers are not used on news programs. The handsome devil with the deep voice and no journalism background is being phased out. With his passing, the straight news writer's job is diminishing—not disappearing altogether, but diminishing. That raises some questions:

- Who is doing the writing?
- What do the writers do?
- What if a person wants to be a broadcast news writer but doesn't want to go on the air?
- Is a writer's job worth struggling for?
- What does it pay?

Increasingly, the writing is being done by the reporters, correspondents, or anchor people themselves—those who not only cover or write the story but also deliver it on the air. It makes sense. The person who covers a story personally will write it better and generally report it better than someone who simply gets facts and notes at his desk and writes a story for someone else to read—or, as it's called, for someone else to voice. Formerly, most copy written by news writers was done for the anchor person. As the quality of broadcast news has been upgraded, the demand has increased for anchor people who also are experienced journalists—that is, people who can write as well as communicate on the air with credibility and authority.

There is, nonetheless, a significant need for news writers who do not want to go on the air or can't go on the air because employers do not want them as on-air correspondents. The bigger the city, the more fierce the competition to be on the air—partly because of ego and partly because of money. At any rate, writers on television news shows enjoy a certain kind of personal freedom not shared by their colleagues on the air. Go into a newsroom in New York and you'll find many writers with big, shaggy beards and wearing the most imaginative (some would say "weird") clothes available. As broadcast news writers they often have a crucial role in what is said and what film goes on the air, but they are not public figures. They enjoy a certain liberating kind of anonymity. Some of them enjoy it immensely. Of course some resent the lack of recognition. Writers' jobs range from the rather tedious to the very challenging; from writing simple headlines to putting together entire news packages.

No news operation has enough reporters or anchor people to cover every story with its own staff members. News stories, unedited film, and tape flow into the newsroom from many sources including the standard news wire services: Associated Press (AP), United Press International (UPI), and Reuters, the British wire.

All wire reports are rewritten: condensed, updated, corrected, and put into a style suitable for broadcasting. That task of condensing, rewriting, expanding to fit film or tape usually is done by news writers.

There are also stories to be gathered from other sources, usually by the news writer working over the phone. There are stories that may be covered by staff reporters who do not have time to come in to write them. As newspaper reporters so often do, they will call in their stories to a writer. They will explain the facts, describe the film or audio tape available to go with the story, and the writer puts the story into words.

At that point he or she is in the position of taking a lot of raw material—facts, film, audio tape, video tape, still pictures—and assembling a final report, deciding what should go where, what portions of film or tape to use to best tell the story. There are stories in which only a film crew (or a single camera person) was on the scene. Then it is up to the writer to look at or listen to what material is available and to put it all together into a coherent news story.

Outside of the daily news shows, writers are used on documentaries. They do the research, write the script, and often double as the producer. Some documentary writer-producers get jobs as free-lancers at the networks and sometimes at large local stations. A good documentary can take a year or more to make, although generally they are budgeted for much less production time.

Writers also function as editors, editing stories written by other writers or reporters. Editors are senior writers who get paid a premium for their work. At the network level, writers are borrowed from the daily news shows for special events, such as space shots, elections, or instant documentaries.

The biggest demand for news writers today is at stations producing daily hour or hour-and-a-half television news shows in the early evening and shorter news programs through the day. In radio the biggest demand is at stations with twenty-four-hour-a-day news formats. The number of those kinds of stations has been growing annually. All network shows employ writers but not a large number of them because so many on-air journalists write their own copy. In between those extremes—the twenty-four-hour-a-day news radio station and the network news show—there are, of course, degrees of need and demand for writers.

Aspiring on-air reporters may wonder if it is necessary to become a news writer first. The answer is very often that there is little choice. Some networks insist that virtually all new people (outside of recognized on-air personalities) start as writers. As a writer, the new person learns the style and format of the program he or she is working on.

It is also a time for employers to get a look at what a person can do. If one can't write well, one's prospects as an on-air reporter are not good.

For a newcomer, a writer's job is excellent training. Broadcast news writers must work fast in order to meet deadlines. They must understand film, editing, audio tape, video tape, and the technique of broadcasting but do not have to worry about going on the air. There is no better starting job, but the pay is surprisingly low. There has always been a mystique about broadcast newsmen, including the conviction that they make more money than print reporters. It is not true. Certain jobs in broadcast news do pay handsomely. The more routine jobs do not. What happened was that as news programs emerged in broadcasting, the industry had to recruit writers who could write news. To do so, the industry paid newspaper reporters and magazine writers more money to come over to broadcasting. The trend did not last.

For example, network broadcast news writers in New York and Washington in 1973 were covered by a union contract that set out a first year minimum of $166 a week. First year reporters at the *New York Times* were also covered by a union contract. Their starting salary was $332.67 a week. After a year and a half a broadcast news writer in New York and Washington was guaranteed $238 a week; the *Times* reporter was earning $334.67. After two years or more (the top scale), broadcast writers got a minimum of $287. The *Times* reporter got $361.67. (Notice, however, that I am comparing news *writers* salaries with newspaper *reporters* salaries. In broadcasting news writers are not reporters. Reporters appear on the air.)

Another important point must be made about broadcast salaries. All editorial jobs in broadcasting are subject to negotiation. What the union contracts guarantee are certain salary minimums. Beyond that, it's every person for himself; what you can bargain for is what you get. If you are trying to break down the employment door to get in, you will probably work for the minimum (or scale) until you prove yourself. If the broadcast employers want you, they'll pay more, and usually do. Some writers make $500, $600, or $700 a week. The majority do not.

Also, first year starting salaries are not really meaningful. Almost no one is hired at the network level as a beginner (or first year) writer. Almost everyone bargains for the top minimum wage to start. If a news writer is not in that bargaining position, the network probably is not interested in him or her anyway.

Moreover, there are all kinds of bonuses. For example, if you are a writer on a network's evening half-hour news show, there is a *commercial* fee. That fee is divided by the two or more writers on the show. The amount of the fees goes up and down depending on the length of the program, from five minutes to over an hour.

Writers who work as editors also get an editor's fee. In 1973 it was an extra $1.40 an hour; or an extra $56 a week for a forty-hour week. Add that to the $287 weekly base, plus overtime, and the network news writer made a good living even in cities as expensive as New York or Washington.

Writers in most major markets are required to join a union;

most of them come under the Writers Guild of America (WGA). The union bargains for the writers and secures company contracts that may last anywhere from one to three years, with annual minimum pay increases written into the contract.

The Assignment Editor

Assignment editors are the unsung heroes of broadcast news. If they do their jobs well, they receive little praise; if they make a mistake, they take a lot of heat. They work strange hours, are not paid enough—and almost always seem to like their jobs.

Assignment editors have a great deal of responsibility. Their decisions are crucial, and they are often forced to make them under the gun—that is, without full knowledge of what they are getting into, without time for consultation. In the long run, a good news operation turns on the abilities of its assignment editors who have neither the prestige of the correspondents nor the power of the producers but the responsibilities of both. However, it is frequently an exciting job. Assignment editors are at the very center of the flow of news and news coverage, and the final product of their judgment is on the air every night. Without a good assignment desk, no news operation can remain competitive for any length of time. There are always lucky breaks, but day in day out, it is the quality of the assignment desk that makes the difference.

- Who are assignment editors and where do they work?
- What do they do?
- What do they get paid?

In large news organizations assignment editors work at a central place known as the assignment desk, which invariably becomes the center of the newsroom action. Because of the immediacy of the job, assignment editors cannot be isolated. Assignment editors generally come from the ranks of news writers. Networks frequently indulge in the luxury of putting good young journalists on the assignment desk to gain experience. It is a luxury because network assignment desks are large and well staffed. A newcomer will not have to work alone. He or she will learn by working with someone who has been around and upon whose judgment one can lean when the situation becomes tense. Smaller operations do not have that kind of manpower and are unwise to put a beginner in such a crucial position. Networks often use the assignment desk: one to handle and coordinate what's going on in the promise can be put, trained, and worked into another job such as field producing or reporting.

Every news operation with its own reporters and technicians has someone who performs the job of assignment editor. Someone has to decide who should go where to cover what stories of the day. Assignment editors do not necessarily make those decisions alone, but they are in charge of seeing that those assignments are carried out and for providing whatever support is necessary to complete them.

In its most basic form a network assignment desk is divided into two parts: foreign and domestic. On any given day there are usually at least four assignment editors working on the desk; one to handle and coordinate what's going on in the United States, one to handle overseas or foreign events, one to work as a backup person to either the foreign or domestic editor, and one to oversee the operation. The back-up person is always free to go into the field as a producer if needed in an emergency.

An assignment desk moves with the flow of news. Some days it is slow. Some days it's hectic—every phone in the house is ringing, bulletins are popping, and the mood and tempo of the desk moves with the action. In New York assignment desks are manned twenty-four hours a day.

Assignment editors start the morning by *reading in,* to find out what has been going on in the world in the sixteen hours they were off shift. At home they begin with the local newspapers. They are listening to the radio news, they are watching the morning television news shows. At work serious reading in begins with wire service copy—AP, UPI, and Reuters—which runs day and night, rolling off the teletype machines, which are constantly stripped and delivered to the assignment editors by desk assistants.

Then, assignment editors must read themselves into what has been done by their own news department: which stories are being covered, which stories are yet to be assigned, which stories are in progress, and what kind of help is likely to be needed to complete those stories and get them on the air.

Wire service reports, newspapers, and other broadcast shows come from the outside, but internally, good news operations also must maintain their own daily log, which is sometimes called a situationer, or troop movements. In the best system I have seen, the situationer, or log, is a mimeographed compilation of anywhere from two to ten or twelve pages. The assignment desk editors keep adding to that log, placing new information at the top and deleting information as assignments are completed or stories are dropped. It is a constant process with each shift making proper additions and deletions and then passing it on to the next shift. The log is mimeographed so that it can be widely distributed throughout the news operation not only to the editors but also to all the producers, correspondents, writers, and so on. Because the log is basically a means of a network news operation keeping track of itself, it includes the following kinds of information:

- The troop movements, which tell where all the company news personnel out covering stories are at any given moment, what they are doing, and where they can be reached;

- Stories that are coming up in the day and must be covered;
- Stories that are coming up in the very near future for which coverage must be planned.

The daily log will also contain other information, details like money orders that have to be sent, arrangements to be made with local stations for coverage or facilities—all the incidentals that otherwise seem to get lost in the press of the day. Finally, a good log has a synopsis of what the other networks are doing on the air, what stories they carried, and what they were about. This synopsis is a monitoring and writing task usually done by the desk assistants.

Items in the log are best broken down geographically, according to where the network bureaus are located—London, Paris, Southeast Asia, New York, Chicago, Los Angeles, and so on. For example, an item on the log under the New York bureau may read:

NEW YORK: PANTHER TRIAL . . . State Court, 100 Centre St., Jackson to meet crew outside courthouse at 9 A.M., film defendants going in, then hooks up with artist for inside sketches, plans on shooting stand-up close at end of day, will advise if wants crew to stand by or come back. Jackson looking for trial wrap-up by 2:30 P.M. Wants courier to meet him at noon break, bring back film and early sketches; he efforting to get interview with Black Panther lawyers at lunch break, if so, courier will stand by until wraps. Show wants for tonite.

It should be noted that not every network keeps the same kind of log. Moreover, local stations usually do not bother to keep such a formal mimeographed compilation since none of their reporters is overseas or generally even out of the state. Local station assignment editors usually keep track of their film crews and reporters on a large blackboard or a plastic sheet on which they write what stories are being covered, who is covering them, and so on. As the day moves on, stories are added and subtracted from the board. Toward the end of the day the news program's producer works from that board to determine what film or tape stories are available for the news program.

Soon after the assignment editor has read in and studied the log, he or she will start getting calls from all over the country—calls from those people listed in the log who are out in the field and have questions, problems, suggestions, or requests. Obviously the assignment editor will have had to study the log carefully to know what they are talking about. The foreign assignment editor has a similar listing of items. However, much of the correspondence is carried on through cables rather than phone, although on the foreign desk one is on the overseas phone much of the day.

The central assignment desk for each of the three networks is in New York, but the assignment editors there do not have to handle all the details personally. They are working with their other network bureaus throughout the country and over-seas. Very often they do not have to do any more than relay interest in a story developing and let the bureau chiefs and assignment editors nearer the story handle it.

For example, let's take a typical Monday in the life of a New York assignment editor. He comes to work in the morning, reads, and gets himself ready for the day.

If the phones aren't ringing when he sits down, he checks his futures file. In that file are kept clippings, notes, mailings, and reminders about events coming up in the next few days or weeks. On this morning he notices that there is a large convention of farmers scheduled in Kansas on Wednesday—two days away. The farmers, about two thousand of them (according to a news release received at the network and filed perhaps two weeks earlier), are angry about farm prices and are meeting to see what they can do. Advance word is that the farmers are really angry and are going to discuss tactics ranging from withholding their products from the market to burning down the White House.

The first thing the editor is likely to do is check with the producers of the various news shows to be sure they are interested in the story and want it covered.

The assignment editor works to supply stories to the news shows. He is working for the producers of those news shows. It is the producers—not the assignment editors—who decide what goes in the air. Let's assume the producers in this case are interested.

The assignment editor now has several options open. Perhaps he feels that the story is exaggerated. Because of past similar meetings, he suspects only fifty farmers are likely to show up instead of two thousand. But he doesn't know for sure, and he wants to keep an eye on developments. He calls the nearest local affiliate in the Kansas area. The news director at the affiliate station says yes, he plans to cover the convention. The New York assignment editor then may make arrangements to have the local man check in with him and cover for the network if anything really happens.

That is the least used option. If a potentially important story is brewing, the network will usually cover it with its own staff. Networks lean on local affiliates in those instances where stories blow up overnight: a riot, an explosion, a flash flood, the unexpected arrival of a dignitary, or the death of a celebrity.

For the Kansas story described, the New York man would call his midwest bureau in Chicago (all three networks have Chicago bureaus) and tell his people there to make arrangements to send a Chicago film crew (usually called the crew —made up of camera, sound, and light persons) and a correspondent to Kansas. The team may also include a field producer to help. Some correspondents prefer to have a field producer accompany them; others do not.

In a sense, then, the story is out of the hands of the New York assignment editor and into the hands of the Chicago bureau. But it never works out that way, entirely, because the final story still has to get to New York for the evening news show on Wednesday. For the moment, however, the New York editor goes on to other worries, and the farmers' convention story is entered in the log as something assigned and being handled by Chicago.

Now comes Wednesday. Let us assume that the farmers are really having a shindig in Kansas. Instead of two thousand, ten thousand show up. Their advance plans generated so much publicity that the president dispatched his secretary of agriculture out there to try to settle the waters. New York and Chicago may discuss the possible need for a second crew. After consulting with the correspondent at the scene, they decide not, but they do decide that the film should be flown directly from Kansas to Chicago because the local station in the area is not able to handle a feed from its facilities. (A feed means taking a network story to a local station, developing and editing the film there, and then electronically feeding the story on a closed circuit into the network.)

It is now up to the New York or Chicago assignment editor to line up a plane, charter it, and arrange for it to be in Kansas and to fly the film to Chicago. Because of the distance, it is possible that he would charter a small jet, costing between $500 and $700 an hour. Sometimes two or even three networks will go in on a pool and share the cost of the charter, but not often. Everyone has different deadlines and problems.

The day moves on, but rarely without problems. Maybe the correspondent calls to say the camera broke down, the sound man is sick, or, typically, the charter didn't show up. Many phone calls follow. The assignment editor calls the charter headquarters and finds out the plane started early and there's still time to divert it to the right Kansas airport.

While all this is going on, of course, the assignment editor has a half dozen other stories cooking, each with its own problems. There are other sources of support for the editor. Networks have transport desks, which handle flight arrangements and film pick-ups, but as time diminishes, the editor will often bypass the transport desk and work directly with the problem at hand, such as a gone-astray airplane.

The correspondent in Kansas may catch the plane and go with it to Chicago with his film, or he may do all he has to do in the field and just send in a recorded script with the film for someone else to edit in Chicago.

Up to this point it is still all rather routine. The plane finds the right airport, and the correspondent is aboard, heading for Chicago. Then a prison riot breaks out in Pennsylvania. A bad one.

The New York assignment editor leaves the Kansas story to the Chicago bureau and swings into Pennsylvania. He has no bureau in Philadelphia. No correspondent in the area. The local affiliated station does not yet have its own people at the scene, and when they do get there, the local news director does not know if they'll have time to cover for the network as well as for its own news show. Through his transport desk, the assignment editor finds out there is a small air strip near the prison.

Another charter is hired (on some days networks may have three or four chartered planes in the sky across the country at the same time). A crew, a film editor, a field producer, and a correspondent are activated from New York. The film editor heads to the local station—probably in Philadelphia— to set up his traveling editing kit. The rest of the crew head for the scene, racing now against the clock.

There are many, many phone calls. The show producers

are calling to see what the assignment editor has arranged; the assignment editor is calling the prison and the local station to see what they've got. When the correspondent from New York touches ground in Pennsylvania, the first thing he or she will do is call the assignment editor to find out what more he has learned. Someone else in the network's traffic department is on the phone making sure there are electronic lines available to make the feed from Philadelphia to New York.

Through it all, the assignment editor has other chores. There are other stories to be arranged, details to be logged, and constant phone calls from all kinds of people asking all kinds of questions.

By the end of the day it may be that the prison riot story could not be gotten in time or that it did come in and ran very long on the air; in fact, so much time was given to the story that the farmers' convention in Kansas (the same story that made it safely to Chicago in time for editing and feeding) was dropped from the news show line-up at the last minute.

Life on the assignment desk is not always like that. There are dead moments. There are also times more hectic than just described. Certain kinds of people enjoy that kind of action, others don't. There is much uncertainty to the job. The assignment editor is very often operating almost in the dark: He gets a call about a prison riot—but is it really a riot or just a momentary disturbance? If he dispatches a large crew for nothing, his bosses will frown; if he misses the story too often, they'll fire him. I am not sure how assignment editors do it, but I do know that the best of them seem to have nothing more scientific than a sixth sense; perhaps it's only from long experience, but they seem to be able to feel out through the telephone wires and judge stories with amazing perception.

Assignment editors also have a good sense of the country,

of distances, geography, contacts, and a notion of what is and what is not possible. Also, they must have a sound knowledge of broadcasting techniques; what it takes to get something done.

Outside of reacting to the immediate flow of daily news events, assignment editors are constantly on the lookout for the unusual and unique, those stories behind the headlines that must be hunted down. In any network there are always more story ideas than crews or air time available to run them. It is part of a selection process, and very often the first screening is done at the assignment editor's desk.

As you'd suspect, an assignment desk is an excellent training ground; it is also a career position if the individual wants to remain in that job. From the assignment desk, editors can move in one of three directions: administration-management; producer; correspondent. The training one gets on the assignment desk (assuming one already has had some writing background) puts an individual in a good position to choose any one of those three courses, depending on interest and talent.

First-rate assignment editors are hard to come by either in a local station or at a network. In 1973 New York network radio and television assignment editors at ABC were paid a base of $333 a week, plus whatever overtime they were asked to work. When they work the overnight shift, they are paid 15 percent more of their salary as a night differential bonus. Assignment editors usually are members of the WGA.

As mentioned earlier, the assignment desk is a good place to gain experience, and some networks use the desk as a spot for someone with promise. In the long run, someone on the assignment desk who is not interested in or not suited for a producer's job or a correspondent's position frequently moves into an administrative-management role. Network radio has similar positions, although the person who does the job of the assignment editor may work under a different title.

At the local level there are many variations on the job. In

a medium-sized city the local television station usually has a full-time assignment editor with a desk manned at least twelve hours a day. The local assignment editor invariably is somebody who knows the city and the surrounding territory well. Of course, the local operation does not have film crews and correspondents running all over the country, but what crews there are must be moved intelligently around the city. Most broadcast news operations, even small ones, function with two-way radios so that the crews in the field can keep in contact with the station.

At small local stations it may be the news director who makes the assignments. After the morning's assignments are made, the news director often goes out as a reporter, leaving a secretary or a film editor or a lab technician to keep track of the phones and news developments. Most local stations monitor the police and fire radios, and they refer constantly to the AP and UPI news wires. If something breaks, the person at the station can get a member of the staff on the two-way radio.

Local assignment editors start at anywhere from $150 to $200 a week and up, depending on one's length of service with the station, the strength of one's personal bargaining position, and the prevailing wage scales at the stations in the area. Increasingly women are coming into the job—something unheard of even in the late 1960s.

The Correspondent

Like Madison Avenue, broadcasting relishes titles. Somewhere along the way, therefore, reporters in network broadcasting became known as correspondents, which sounds more impressive than reporter. For years major newspapers have used the title correspondent for reporters on the staff who work away from the newspaper's main office. That may include a suburban staff correspondent, for example, or a foreign correspondent in Greece. Broadcasting made no such distinction. One reason is that network reporters are away from their headquarters most of the time. The other reason is that broadcasters love titles.

CBS, however, has two categories of journalists: reporters and correspondents. In effect, reporters are junior correspondents. Most journalists who are on the air are correspondents; even anchor people are known officially as correspondents. At most local stations reporters are still called reporters, or street reporters.

Street reporter is a good term. Television and radio reporters spend a good deal of their time on the street—interviewing, covering demonstrations, riots, rallies, murders, whatever is occurring "out there" in the street. It can be an exhausting job filled with frustrations and complications. Print reporters don't share many of those problems because they are not saddled with the electronic gear, technical problems, and logistics. A television reporter's camera has been called his two-ton pencil.

Comparatively, correspondents are paid well for their frustrations. At the local station level a broadcast reporter generally is paid more than his or her counterpart at the local newspaper, but the salary range varies greatly. A street reporter in Boston makes twice the salary of a street reporter in Miami. The difference depends upon management, the size of the market, an area's prevailing wage scales, and an individual's ability to negotiate a salary. Generally only reporters in the larger markets are covered by a union contract that establishes minimum salaries.

People who are on the air in either television or radio are known as talent. A director in the studio may ask, for example, "Who's the talent today?" He means, who's going to be on camera. CBS news correspondent Walter Cronkite is the talent for the CBS Evening News program.

Describing a reporter as the talent is indicative of the

curious marriage broadcasting has made between journalism and show business. It also helps to explain the kind of union broadcast reporters are in. Years ago, television and radio performers realized that they had good reason to band together in a union for mutual bargaining strength. They formed what has evolved into the American Federation of Radio and Television Artists, commonly known as AFTRA.

When broadcast news people came along, there were too few of them to form much of a union on their own. The journalists. therefore, joined AFTRA. Today, news persons working on the air are paid somewhat the same as actors and actresses. They are paid a base salary plus fees for every time they appear on the air.

The pay scales for news talent can become very complicated. In 1973 the basic salary, or *guarantee* for a network correspondent was $410 a week, plus fees. That was the minimum. Many correspondents negotiate much better deals. A network anchor person with a big following can get in the neighborhood of $250,000 or $300,000 a year. Most of the major correspondents have agents who do the bargaining for them. Agents get anywhere from a straight 10 percent of the annual wage, or less, depending on the arrangement worked out beforehand. Some agents also serve as business managers, handling a correspondent's taxes and investments as well as contract negotiations and complaints.

Most seasoned correspondents at the network level do not work for the $410-plus-fees minimum scale, but a newcomer anxious to break into the business as a correspondent usually is offered and accepts the AFTRA minimum.

Most local broadcast stations outside of the biggest cities do not pay their correspondents any fees. Instead, they work on a flat salary. Some stations pay overtime; some do not.

Putting money aside, what does a broadcast reporter do and what does it take to be one?

The textbooks of journalism often discuss the six little

helpers, the Who, What, When, Where, Why, and How of news: the questions that must be answered in any news report. But if simply answering those questions was all there was to reporting, almost anyone could be trained to be a reporter. It is much more than that. As society becomes increasingly complex, it becomes increasingly clear that journalism that stops at the six little helpers is not enough.

For example, a news story reports that automation is taking over tobacco picking. What does that mean to all the people who used to do the jobs that the machines are going to do? Does it mean we can expect a large migration from the tobacco farms to the cities? If so, what cities? And what are those cities doing to prepare for it? Journalism cannot satisfy itself with simply reporting the facts and not giving some idea of what they mean. The profession and the industry must develop and reward reporters who display the intellectual ability to seize a story, think it through, and consider its most meaningful elements beyond the obvious.

What about physical attributes? Obviously, not all broadcast reporters have to have beautiful voices and look like movie stars. Broadcast news has come a long way from those days. Ironically enough, the best news operations have gotten the farthest from it. At those places, correspondents are as prized for their intelligence as for their looks or camera style.

There are limits, of course. One's speaking voice cannot be a high squeak, a barely audible whisper, a deadly monotone, or have an irritating twang. But almost any conversational tone with the words comfortably and clearly articulated and the voice reasonably modulated is acceptable on the air.

For the beginning broadcast reporter, the problem most often is not the conversational voice, but the speaking voice— that phony elocution and two-tones-lower-than-normal voice that comes out when the person gets in front of a microphone.

It is very much like putting a beginning writer in front of

a typewriter. He or she can write a wonderfully natural, informal letter in longhand to a friend, but once in front of a typewriter that person becomes a *Writer:* Everything comes out frozen and stiff. It is not easy to be comfortable in front of a microphone, certainly not in the beginning. The object for any beginner is to learn to relax and speak naturally instead of "professionally." An audience listening to or watching a newscast does not want to be lectured to; it wants to be informed.

In terms of looks, it's more a question of presence than physical appearance. An audience responds to someone with a sense of poise and composure and warmth. It will turn off someone who appears embarrassed. It also will turn off a reporter or anchor person who comes on like a Shakespearean actor.

The ability to relax in front of a microphone or on camera comes easier to some than others. But it is never easy in the beginning. And getting good at it is almost always a question of experience—of going on the air 500 times. Then it gets easier.

I am frequently asked about those announcing schools advertised in the backs of big city newspapers. They are not recommended for broadcast reporters. Perhaps they are useful for aspiring disc jockeys or staff announcers, but genuine news organizations are not looking for announcers, they're looking for journalists.

I am asked also about newspaper training. The basics of journalism are the same no matter what the medium: print or electronic. As a matter of fact, for practical, preliminary training, newspapers are fine places to start. Beginning print reporters get more practice writing than broadcast reporters because it takes a lot more stories to fill a newspaper. The written copy for an entire half-hour evening news program on any network does not fill a single page of the *New York Times.*

On the other hand, the broadcast reporter does function as something more than a reporter with a pad and pencil. The broadcast reporter must know how to combine news content with the technology necessary to tell the story through the electronic medium. In other words, the broadcast reporter functions not only as a reporter but also as a producer and sometime technician.

The *sometime* depends upon how much help is available. In many small stations the reporter is also the camera person, the film editor, and everything else nobody else is there to do. But whether one works in a big or little station, the broadcast reporter must understand the basic theory behind all of the equipment, even if he or she does not know how, actually, to operate all the gear.

The television reporter usually directs the film crew or at least gives the members of the crew a clear idea of what is needed on film to tell the story. The same is true of the radio reporter with a tape recorder, although radio reporters can do the recording themselves on portable recorders.

Sometimes it is perfectly obvious what should be filmed. Sometimes it is not. The difficulty comes in figuring out what will be needed before the news report is written. That requires a conception of film and tape production. It is not like writing a movie, because ninety-nine times out of a hundred the reporter cannot go back and film or record the news story over again. One either gets it on film or tape when it happens or misses it forever.

Problems arise when the correspondent's script does not match the film or audio tape. The correspondent, for example, may be reporting on a scene of great chaos, but the only film he or she got at the scene is one of calm and quiet. Sometimes the script has to be written out in the field, recorded there, and sent in with the film or tape.

Preferably, the correspondent returns to the station with the material, screens or listens to it before writing the script, and then joins the written words to the material so that they fit the pictures or sound.

The chore is always one of condensing the report. After spending anywhere from several hours to several days on a story, it is painful to cut and boil down the final product to a report that runs a minute and a half or two or three minutes, rarely more.

Clearly a broadcast reporter must know his or her way around the technology of broadcasting. One must understand the editing process. One must learn how to pull it all together with a script. All that requires a degree of imagination and technical awareness combined with writing ability and poise on the air. But if there is any single trait that no correspondent can do without, I'd have to say that one trait is persistence; the endurance and drive necessary to get the job done. The hours a broadcast correspondent works are remarkably long, and the pressure is always there. The frustrations are enormous, and the next day is only hours away.

Broadcast news seems to have no yesterdays. News directors never are very interested in what a correspondent did yesterday. They don't want to hear about yesterday's eighteen-hour day. What they do want to know is, "What have you done for me today?"

The Producer

Producer is an umbrella title. There are all kinds of producers, ranging from Hollywood wizards who may do nothing more than raise money, to news producers who do the writing, directing, editing, and producing as well. In effect, producers are defined by what and how they produce— whether it's a daily news show, a documentary, a special event, a variety show, or a movie. It depends a lot on an individual producer's talent and preference.

In news, for example, many documentary producers have

discovered that they are not very good when it comes to putting together daily news shows. (Daily news shows that go on the air at the same time every day, in the the same time strip Monday through Friday, are called strip shows.)

Strip show producers, accustomed to the daily action and pressure, may become bored spending six or eight months producing a single documentary. Some producers are good administrators but are not very handy when it comes to going out in the field to get material.

At the local station level the distinctions between various kinds of producers are not carefully drawn. There, producers frequently double as on-air reporters, anchor people, even as camera people. But at some point a person must decide between being a producer or an on-air reporter. At the network level the line between producer and correspondent is clear and only rarely crossed. Although a correspondent frequently functions as a producer in the field, producers do not function as correspondents.

Producers generally come from the ranks of writers or assignment editors, production assistants, or assistants to the producers. At the network they also may come from local stations, where they have distinguished themselves as news directors or local producers.

Their salaries and contracts are negotiated individually. There is no set rate. Again, at the network level, producers' salaries range from $15,000 to $125,000 a year, depending upon experience, accomplishment, and demand for an individual's talent. There are three broad categories: associate producer, producer, and executive producer.

ASSOCIATE PRODUCER

Associate producers start at somewhere between $15,000 and $20,000 a year depending on their individual contracts. Associate producers frequently are called field producers, because they may spend most of their time out in the field with engineers or camera crews and correspondents. Field producers work long hours but generally receive only flat wages with no overtime consideration. Except in a few cases in some areas, they are considered part of management and do not belong to a union.

An associate producer also may spend most of his or her time in the newsroom. Under a senior producer, the associate producer works on editing and putting together reports sent in from the field by camera crews and correspondents. Radio does not generally make extensive use of producers. Radio correspondents most often do both jobs. It is easier for them because they do not have large crews of technicians to worry about. Those who do function as producers in radio may do so under some other title. At any rate, in giving titles, the term *associate producer* is not generally used. It is used more for pay purposes than description. Associate producers are generally just called producers.

It is up to the associate producer working back at the station to take a great deal of raw material and to edit it into one package. The object is to blend the correspondent's recorded report with appropriate film or audio tape, video tape, slides, still pictures, graphics, or whatever material is available to tell the story. When a producer is doing that job, he or she is working as an in-house producer.

Most associate producers prefer to work in the field because that is where the action is. But what does one do in the field?

If a producer goes out without a correspondent—that is, with only a film crew—it is up to him or her to decide what should be filmed, what speeches or action should be recorded. At that point, the producer is the boss.

When the field producer comes back to the station with an enormous amount of raw material, a correspondent may be asked to screen the film or listen to the tape, discuss it, and determine how it should be edited. The correspondent then writes and narrates the story, and the producer edits it. There are many field producers who work that way—those who dig up a story, go out and get it, and bring it back to work with a correspondent on its final presentation. Generally, those are features or background stories or investigative kinds of reports. Those stories may require a lot of time and digging but not a correspondent on the scene to appear on camera or to do interviews.

The field producer may also go out into the field with a correspondent. It could be that the producer is the one who researched the story, set up the contacts, and made the arrangements. Or the producer may be just assisting the correspondent who did all that. Some television correspondents are better reporters than producers; they are not as skilled in the technical film or tape production required to capture a story. In that case the producer handles filming and editing direction, and the correspondent handles the reporting.

More often than not, a field producer accompanies the correspondent into the field when a story has to be done rapidly and brought back to a local station for feeding to the network. Then the producer worries not only about helping to get the story but also about the dozens of technical aspects involved: constant communication with the network producers, arranging electronic lines to feed the report into the network, being sure the film gets processed and edited properly, working out the logistics of airline schedules, charters or couriers. During those times the correspondent has enough to do just figuring out what the story is about, what should be written or told, and getting the basic questions asked and answered before the report goes on the air. The producer handles the rest.

Throughout the entire process the field producer functions as a journalist as well as a coordinator. The producer is expected to be knowledgable not only with film but also with the requirements of live broadcasting as well. When things go wrong, when reports do not make the air, when equipment fails to function because it was not properly checked or placed, it is usually the field producer who takes the blame. Good field producers are totally flexible and, like assignment editors, often are called upon to make judgments that involve a good deal of guessing about developments over which they have no control.

Field producers generally move up to become senior producers—but not always. Some don't want to. They prefer traveling and the action in the field.

SENIOR PRODUCER

Not all news operations make the distinction between field producer and senior producer. It may be only a question of money. Senior producers at the network rarely make less than $30,000 a year, and most make more. As a rule senior producers do not travel as much as associate producers. They are more securely held down to positions involving a larger view of news production. For example, a senior producer on a network evening news show may be supervising the work of a half dozen field producers.

Network documentaries are almost always produced by full producers. Where an associate producer may be responsible for only parts of a program, a full producer is responsible for the entire program.

The producing corps, then, is pyramidal, beginning with associate producers who work under senior producers who usually report to an executive producer.

EXECUTIVE PRODUCER

In broadcasting, the executive producer is as high as one goes in the producing ranks. Executive producers answer to vice presidents and presidents of network news. Executive producers responsible for influential network news programs are paid handsomely (from $75,000 to $125,000 a year, not including fringe benefits). Executive producers almost always make more money than their administrative bosses. At CBS, when Fred Friendly was promoted from his position as executive producer of the documentary series "CBS Reports" to become president of CBS News, he had to take a $25,000 cut in pay. The logic, apparently, is that one job involves producing, the other administration, and it's easier to find a good administrator than a top producer. For that matter, in the business world star salesmen can make more money than their bosses.

The best producer's job in network news is executive producer of the nightly news show. *Best* may not be the right word; traditionally it has been the most powerful and prestigious position. Few men have ever held that job for five years in a row. Maybe no man should. The pressures are too great, and over a period of time there is a tendency to go stale, to take fewer risks, to lose one's competitive edge. Whether it's a space shot, a documentary, or a daily news program, the executive producer contends with everything: management's displeasure, technical failure, talent failure, personality squabbles, and budgets.

As a man I worked under for several years put it, there is no one way—*no right or wrong way*—to produce a news program. It is up to a producer's peers, audience, and critics to judge whether a program has been done well. It is a matter of taste, judgment, competition, and, often, luck.

There is in all of broadcasting an element of group journalism; normally one person cannot do all that is required to produce even a single television report or (to a lesser degree) radio report. On the other hand, a daily news program cannot be produced by a committee. At some point one person must make the decisions on what stories are going to be placed in the program, where they will be placed, and how long they will run. That is the executive producer's job. To make those three decisions successfully every day takes a lot of authority, talent, work, and nerve.

An executive producer proceeds in much the same way as a conductor of a symphony. The producer orchestrates the news program. A conductor deals in sound. An executive producer deals in time. Producers orchestrate time. If it's a half-hour nightly news program, they are faced with a time slot that must begin and end on the split second. If it's a one-hour documentary time slot, there is no more time than just that—one hour minus commercials, of course.

It is a process of elimination. The executive producer of any news program, whether it is a network show or a local production, works with many others. All of those people want to get their material on the air, but time is limited. It is up to the executive producer to make the final decisions concerning what goes in and what doesn't. Making those kinds of judgments is what the executive is paid for and what he or she is judged by. It is the executive producer who is responsible for the total program: Does it hang together? Is it paced well? Does it make sense? Is it accurate? Is it competitive with the other news programs?

The lament of the executive producer has to do with the number of people he or she must rely on. If they fail, the executive producer takes the ultimate responsibility. But much of what happens is out of the executive's direct control. Very often it is the person in the field who makes the initial decisions that affect the final outcome. If the reporter does something stupid, there's not much the executive producer can do once the story has passed.

For that reason, executive producers are constantly consulted on major decisions—no matter what time or where. Like a doctor, the executive producer of a daily news program goes nowhere without leaving a phone number. Major amounts of staff time and company money ride on the executive's decisions, which must often be made over the phone in the middle of the night.

Finally, executive producers do not simply put together news programs out of all the available stories presented to them. To be good, they must be innovators. They must generate story ideas, dozens of them every week.

It is the executive producer who sets the pace for the news program. In small and even medium-sized stations it is often the news director who serves as the executive producer. But whatever the title, successful executive producers must be able to establish their authority and to command respect.

In short, it is the executive producer who urges employees to be bold, to take chances, to come up with the unexpected —to think originally. And it is the executive producer who puts it all together, who gives a program an identifiable pace, style, and format instead of presenting a grab bag of bits and pieces of news thrown together at the end of a day.

That's why top grade executive producers are paid so much and are so hard to find.

6

Where and
How to Start

The best place to start a career in broadcast journalism is at a local commercial station. If you have no professional experience, your starting job is likely to be menial and poorly paid.

If your job search is truly a beginning venture, look for a station small enough or without rigid union jurisdictions so that you'll have a wider range of responsibilities and the greatest chance for exposure to a number of work experiences. Most of the time a small station will afford you the chance to do more sooner.

Do not fear being stuck there forever. Moving from job to job as one's skill increases is a traditional part of building a journalism career. Starting is most important. In the beginning your interest should be directed toward gaining credentials and experience. Money and fame can come later.

Is that easier said than done? How hard is it to get a job in broadcast journalism? There is always a degree of luck involved, of being in the right place at the right time. But let's consider newspapers for a moment.

Newspapers are a lot more familiar to us than broadcasting. Most young journalists are fairly confident that if they really wanted to go into newspaper work, they could find a job. If that confidence is realistic, and I think it is, consider the numbers—that should give an indication of the chances for getting a job in broadcast journalism.

There are roughly 1,750 daily newspapers in the United States. A survey conducted by the Department of Labor in 1972 on the job market for print reporters predicted that there would be job openings for 1,650 new reporters every year until at least 1980. The survey did not concern itself with broadcast journalists, but other sources reveal that compared to the 1,750 daily newspapers in the country, there are 6,530 commercial radio stations and nearly 700 commercial television stations. Also, there are 446 public or educational radio stations and 196 public television stations. That totals up to more than 7,800 stations on the air today.

Some of these stations have little money and few employees. Some don't do much in news and would be able to offer only limited job experience. But somewhere in one of those 7,800 stations there is a need and an opening for a bright beginner. The object is to find the station. How?

Every year *Broadcasting* magazine publishes the *Broadcasting Yearbook*. It will not tell you which station is looking for journalists or technicians, but it will tell you where the stations are. It contains a brief fact sketch of every commercial broadcasting operation in the United States, Canada, Mexico, and the Caribbean. It lists every radio and television station in this country by state, including the names of the stations' owners, program directors, and news directors, along with the stations' call letters, addresses, and phone numbers. (Be careful about addressing letters by name. The broadcast business is subject to rapid turnover. It is best to use a personal name, but be sure it is correct. Otherwise, just address a letter to the proper title, such as News Director.) The publication also lists colleges that have broadcast stations. The yearbook also may help in writing term papers or supplying background material on the history of broadcasting. It includes a good but brief history of the industry, its rules and regulations. Information about where to get the publication is given on page 150.

The weekly *Broadcasting* magazine and the monthly *Editor and Publisher* magazine regularly list some broadcast news job openings. Except for a very few specialized places, personnel agencies usually do not have listings for broadcast news openings. Personnel agencies in the big cities do have listings sometimes for jobs in film or tape production houses, which may be of interest to some.

The Radio and Television News Directors Association (RTNDA), a national organization, maintains a clearing-house for employment opportunities, but it is designed more for experienced broadcast news people.

Overall, broadcast managers do not advertise widely when looking for journalists. They rarely have to, because they are always receiving resumes, which they keep on file. Also, they usually know where to look for the particular kinds of employees they need—often no farther than across the street at their competitor's operation. Broadcasters have no reluctance to raid another station's staff if they can.

Generally, journalists are not hired by personnel departments. They are hired by other news people, such as the managing editor or a news director or an executive producer. Hiring a journalist has a lot to do with being able to judge his or her instincts or promise. That is best conveyed in a personal interview. An applicant should always try to secure a personal appointment. That is not always possible, either because the station is too far away or because the news director does not see anyone until first receiving a résumé and an audition tape.

One tries to secure a personal interview in any way possible: a phone call, a letter followed up by a phone call, a friend's introduction, and so on. With or without an immediate interview (hopefully to sell oneself as a bright, eager, invaluable addition to the station's news staff), one most likely will be asked for a résumé and perhaps be asked to do an on-the-spot audition.

A good résumé or audition may help one get in the door. A résumé or an application form gives an employer a quick look at a prospective employee's credentials and provides some basis for judging a person's promise or ability to fit into the news operation. With a beginner that judgment has to be based largely on promise, since he or she does not yet have much demonstrable experience.

In job-hunting, always treat yourself kindly. After making a realistic appraisal of your abilities and promise, assume the reason somebody does not hire you has more to do with his particular needs than with your shortcomings. Never forget that the person interviewing you for a job was once in the same position.

You must, of course, have some reasonable credentials—preferably an academic background combined with some practical beginning experience. That experience may be nothing more than work in a school station or a part-time job in some journalistic enterprise, but at least it's something to put down on a résumé.

When writing a résumé, go with your strength. In the news business, as with most other occupations, job experience and performance are more important than scholastic credits. But if you have little practical journalism experience and a good deal of education, emphasize your impressive educational background. There are entire books in any library on how to write résumés. A wise employer, or one skilled in reading résumés, will figure out where you are anyway, but there's no sense in emphasizing one's deficiencies. That's up to the man with the job opening to determine. And a bright novice is more valuable than a tired hack.

Sometimes even a brief résumé can be embarrassing because there is no work experience to put down. In that case, a personal letter might be best. It should state what you would like to do, why you selected that station, and a brief description of your background and your willingness to work. It may help to accompany your letter with a letter of recommendation from a school counselor or a friend who may have some influence.

After a résumé or letter has been sent or personally dropped off at a news director's office, it is a good idea to follow up with a phone call after a week or so asking for a personal appointment. Follow-up calls really amount to a request for a reaction. In effect the caller is saying, "You've seen my résumé; what do you think, will you see me?" Of course, the caller never puts it that bluntly and the employer rarely responds with total candor.

Ideally, the employer says, "Yes, I read your résumé, your credentials look good. When can you come to work?" But it rarely works that way. At best, the employer agrees to a personal appointment. But he or she might say, "Yes, I read your résumé. You don't have much experience, do you?" or, "Why didn't you finish college?"

It is at that point that job-hunting becomes something more than just knocking on doors and sending out résumés. It is at that point one begins selling oneself.

"No sir," the quick-witted applicant replies over the phone, "I haven't finished yet. But I'm really interested in broadcasting. I'd like to get a start on it, and I think I can prove myself." And so on.

Auditions or samples of one's work can accompany the résumé or come afterward. Auditions, which are called air checks, are good points of departure in the process of getting a job. One can control the quality of an audition by doing it by oneself, or an audition can be arranged at the station where one applies. It depends a lot on what kind of job one is applying for.

For prospective editorial employees there is usually a writing test. An applicant is given a packet of Associated Press or United Press International news wire copy and asked to rewrite the copy into a five-minute news program.

Generally applicants are given as much wire copy as they want. They go through the copy, select a number of stories, and write them into a single package. Applicants usually worry a lot about selecting only the most important stories and about putting them in just the right order. The fact is, the employer rarely notices or cares about that.

The test is designed to give the employer an idea of the applicant's ability to write for broadcasting—to write for the ear rather than the eye. Most important is how the applicant tackles the job and how it sounds when he or she is through. Sometimes a person is given a time limit for completing the test. Generally nobody takes that seriously unless the applicant does something extraordinary, like knock off the test effortlessly in ten minutes, or take four hours for what should be a one- or two-hour process.

After writing the test, the job-hunter often is asked to record it on audio or video tape, which may not make much sense if the applicant is not seeking a job as an on-air news reporter. Assignment editors, researchers, and many other broadcast news personnel do not go on the air. But the "write it–read it" test is the traditional trial at local stations. It is quick. It is easy to administer. It gives the employer a chance to see how a prospective employee works under at least some pressure and how he or she looks on camera or sounds on radio. Unfortunately the test does not measure an applicant's ability to work in the field, or one's effectiveness in dealing with the technology of broadcasting.

Beginners usually are not required to take a test if the job in question is clearly a menial one, but one cannot stay in a beginner's job forever, and preparation for such testing is good discipline. At the network level, tests or auditions often are more realistic, tailored to try applicants in the job categories they are seeking.

Once they get a start, beginning journalists have a tendency to move around a lot. During their early career years journalists are likely to change jobs every two or three years from a smaller station to a bigger station—perhaps in the same state or maybe to a station across the country.

There's a value to being exposed to different news operations. Each one does things differently, some better than others. For example, there is one station in Arkansas whose editing room is set up entirely backwards. Normally, film rewind and splicing procedures are done working from left to right. But the first man who worked there started from scratch. He taught himself how to edit. He did it backwards, and that's how everyone who came along afterwards learned from him.

In broadcasting there is an informal grapevine about news job openings. The process of moving around reflects a beginning journalist's growing awareness of what's going on in the industry. Gradually he or she makes connections. The grapevine begins feeding information about openings or better working conditions somewhere else. As a person gets better at a job, he or she becomes increasingly attractive on the job market. Other stations are willing to pay more or to offer greater responsibilities.

There is always a demand somewhere for a good, experienced broadcast journalist; and at some point the journalist decides where he or she wants to be. That may not happen until he or she finally moves to a network job. Of course, some people move from job to job at the same station. They may remain at the station where they started because it is a good place to work in a community that is a good place to live. What most journalists want, whether on the local or network level, is a job with a good-sized station committed to news—a station that pays adequately, allows for expansion, rewards merit, and provides incentive.

Getting a job at the network level is similar to getting a job at a station in a major market, only it's more difficult. Every year the three networks receive thousands of applications, résumés, and general pleas for work. Obviously thousands of jobs are not available. However, there are always some jobs available; yet most applicants are turned down. Why? The networks are looking for experienced, "known" personnel for the higher level positions. Networks are reluctant to take chances with newcomers, untrained or unknown at the network or major market level. Yet, obviously, there are some jobs available.

In any organization the size of a network someone is always leaving, being promoted, being transferred, taking a leave of absence, getting sick, or getting fired. Also, new positions are being created or opened up after having gone unfilled for budget reasons.

The criterion for hiring is performance. One does not have to know someone in the usual job-hunting sense of the phrase. The stakes are too high for news executives to hire an unqualified person for a meaningful job at the network just to do someone a favor.

You do not have to know someone, but you are not likely to get hired unless someone in the network knows your work. Network personnel travel around the country with the flow of news and frequently work with local stations. Network people are always on the phone making arrangements for spot coverage, local facilities, or whatever. A particularly competent local producer becomes known and is depended upon; an especially alert local assignment editor is trusted; a good local correspondent occasionally is given the chance to do reports that run on the network.

One way or another, one becomes known. These people become the successful applicants for network jobs. For the unknown, it almost never happens, although some fortunate few have been hired as they walked in the door—a question of luck and timing.

Years ago Walter Cronkite in an article in *Quill* magazine, said, "We have some bright young men and women in CBS News who came up through the copy boy (or girl) route, but it takes exceptional people to do that successfully, because the truth is we don't yet have the means to train them from scratch." He said that in 1962. It is still true.

There is also a human element in network employment practices. Because pressure is on for performance, the inclination is to go with experience instead of risking failure with someone untried. For example, one network for years told applicants that they would be considered only after they had five years of experience in a major market. That was never quite true. If someone came along who proved he or she was good enough, no one quibbled about how many years someone had worked where.

There is also the problem of job classification. News people in network radio and television are required to join the appropriate unions. Jobs are strictly classified: writer, correspondent, editor, producer, camera person, film editor, and so on. Even the copy boys (desk assistants) are represented by unions.

Each job has a negotiated, minimum union pay scale. Minimums work to the advantage of those already on the payroll, but they are a disadvantage to someone breaking in because the rigid job classification tends to create barriers. Even if a sympathetic network executive wanted to give a newcomer a try, he could not do it unless that individual joined the right union and thereafter was paid the union scale. At the network, therefore, one does not break in a promising desk assistant by giving him or her a chance to do some reporting on the air now and then. To do so, the desk assistant would have to join the union and be paid accordingly. One could not be a desk assistant and a part-time reporter. The same union jurisdiction rules apply to most major stations.

The safest approach for the person doing the hiring at the network and major station level, then, is to go for experience.

The hazard to that approach is obvious: Experience does not mean talent. Someone with experience may be simply someone who has learned to do the job routinely rather than well or imaginatively. There are hacks in all professions. Certainly they exist in broadcast journalism—and some of them at the highest levels.

There is another barrier for the newcomer to the network, a less formal barrier than union restrictions, but still formidable. The network news industry is an incestuous kind of business. There are thousands of bars and restaurants in New York, but during off-hours, television and radio news people gather in roughly six of them. The establishments themselves are never owned by the networks, but they become part of the industry. (At the time of John Kennedy's assassination, for example, all three networks were dispatching personnel all over the country. At three o'clock, the banks closed. Personnel needed expense money in cash. Late in the afternoon the ABC cashier's office ran out of cash. The owner of the local bar where ABC personnel congregate came through for a quick loan of $7,500 in cash.)

When news people gather socially they usually talk shop. They exchange information on what is going on—who is leaving, who is coming, what new programs are being planned. Word on openings or changes are heard frequently by lowly staff members even before many of the top executives hear of them. And in the network, most hiring is controlled from New York, even if the job involved is in a bureau in Rome or Saigon or Cleveland.

With that kind of efficiency in internal communications, coupled with the instincts of network executives to hire experience, the newcomer trying to get in is clearly at a disadvantage. Nonetheless, newcomers are hired all the time. But they are newcomers to the network, *not* to broadcasting. Almost always they have proved themselves somewhere else first.

To sum up, then, the beginning broadcast journalist should get experience wherever possible. Even a local newspaper makes sense as a starting place. The goal is to learn the business of journalism, to gain credentials, and to keep looking for an opening. Good journalists are always in demand somewhere.

Since the object is to get one's work recognized, it does not matter where one starts. A small commercial station often provides the best kind of experience because the newcomer will have the opportunity to do many jobs that are not possible in bigger stations.

And the beginner must be aware that beginning is the hardest part. No one likes to job hunt. But it is unlikely anyone is going to *offer* a beginner a job. Nothing happens until one asks, and usually, nothing happens until one asks in dozens of places. Persistence is a basic part of the journalist's makeup.

There is the true story of one of the two young *Washington Post* reporters who originally broke open the Watergate scandal. He was working for a small nearby paper, but he wanted desperately to work for the *Post*. The managing editor of the *Post* didn't think he had enough experience. The young man wouldn't take no for an answer. He kept calling. The managing editor kept saying no.

Finally, one day the editor was home painting his roof. The phone rang. It was for him. He climbed down the ladder and came to the phone. It was the young fellow, still asking for a job.

In a rage the editor said *no!* His wife overheard the conversation and noted that persistent young reporters like that seemed to be what the editor said he was always looking for. The editor got to thinking about that—and finally hired the young man.

Shortly thereafter the *Washington Post* won a Pulitzer Prize for its coverage of Watergate.

7

Which Is Better,
Network or Local?

For the beginner, the question of which is better may be ridiculous, or at least premature. Beginners start wherever they can, and nobody at a network is going to offer a beginner a truly meaningful job. But sooner or later in one's career the question may very well come up, and it is helpful to have some idea at the outset whether network employment is a reasonable or even a desirable goal.

But isn't this like asking an aspiring young actress which she would prefer, the hometown little theater or Broadway? Or asking the baseball player, which is better, the farm team or the majors?

No. It is not. There is an important difference, and it will help to recognize this difference right at the beginning because it might save a lot of frustration in later years.

First, one must recognize the American ethic; the belief that bigger is better, that success means moving onward and upward, that careers are divided between the big leagues and the little leagues. By that reasoning, electronic journalism at the local station level is the little league and the network is the big league. In two books I read on journalism careers (both written by former newspaper reporters who never worked in broadcasting), both described the networks as the big leagues.

It is not true. Network and local news are two different kinds of leagues. They should not be compared. A career in either one has its own kinds of rewards, satisfactions, and frustrations.

I know several prominent local station journalists who have turned down network job offers. Why? Are they ignorant or lazy? No. They have their share of the driving ambition that so often characterizes broadcast journalists. They have been around the industry long enough to know what it's all about. But after looking over both fields, they decided that life at the network level was not for them—mentally, physically, even financially. (Most local anchor people and major reporters in the big cities make more money than the average network correspondent. Some local anchor people in cities like New York, Chicago, and Los Angeles make $100,000 to $150,000 a year.)

The financial curve of the broadcast journalist does not follow the trajectory of the baseball rookie who starts on a farm team, makes $500 a month, and rides all night from stadium to stadium in an old school bus, dreaming of the day when he can fly first class with the big leaguers. When it comes to the simple comforts—like home, car, bank account, and working conditions—established local reporters in major markets live better than the average network correspondent, producer, or editor.

There is also the question of recognition. Journalists, like other human beings, appreciate recognition. They want the largest audience possible to see and hear their reports. It would seem, therefore, that the place to be is a network where a nightly news program is seen by millions. Personal recognition and appreciation for one's work, however, is not necessarily based on the size of the audience. There are very few national news stars immediately recognizable by the public.

The few there are spent fifteen to twenty years getting there. In terms of recognition, they are in their prime, but most of them also are moving toward the end of their careers. The prime time of a person's career in broadcasting frequently does not coincide with the prime years of his or her life.

The fact is that the local reporter can have a far greater impact on his community than the overwhelming majority of network journalists. The local reporter's findings often result in immediate response. Moreover, local reporters receive a far greater degree of direct respect and appreciation in their communities.

Most network newsmen trudge along somewhere between stardom and oblivion. Occasionally they receive some minor portion of national recognition usually lavished on anchor people, but not often. Ego rewards are relative; some need them more than others. For those who do best with a great deal of personal recognition, a good local station provides a much better opportunity for receiving it. In many places the local television reporter is better known than virtually anyone else in town.

It gets down to the simple question of lifestyle. What kind of area does one prefer to live in? A good, experienced broadcast journalist generally can choose the spot. It may be a big city or a relatively small town; it depends on his or her preference. But network employees do not always have that latitude. In the beginning, at least, they go where the network sends them.

There is the question of job availability. There are thousands of local broadcast reporters. There are roughly only 150 network television correspondents for all of the three networks. The fact is, then, that no matter what the personal desires (and in some cases, no matter what the talent), most broadcast journalists will not become network correspondents. There are not enough jobs to go around. That may be a blessing. There are many, many examples of the first-rate local reporter who did poorly or was not happy as a national correspondent. There are many local reporters who went through all the frustrations and pressures it takes to become a network employee only to discover the network was not for them. That does not mean they were not good at their jobs. It means some people work better in one kind of operation than others. It may have something to do with the different kinds of pressure. It may have to do with the question of group journalism. There is more pressure and a lot more group journalism at the network level. Some people do well under pressure—even thrive on it; others do not, or at least not the kind of pressure at the network level that often overflows with administrators, some of whose demands can exceed good sense or fairness.

There are those, however, who will never be happy until they are working at the network level. That desire has more to do with personality than professional ability, but there are two major attractions offered the network journalist:

- Quality story assignments
- Extensive technical facilities and technicians

By their nature, national story assignments usually are more varied, almost always more challenging, and more keenly competitive than local station assignments. Network stories are not necessarily more meaningful—just bigger.

Also, on a comparative basis, networks spend a lot of money covering news. They have to if they are going to remain competitive. If they do not, the ratings go down, sponsors lose interest, and the network loses money. The same argument, of course, can be made at the local level, but local owners do not always see it that way.

Many network newsmen are comfortable only with the extensive facilities of a large operation. They find it hard to function without the services of the most skilled technicians in the industry.

On the other side, local reporters often complain about the kinds of stories they are required to cover. They naturally object to being asked to use their skills covering a supermarket opening because the place might become a big advertiser. They object to covering ceremonial, nonsense functions of local dignitaries or corporate powers or publicity hungry civic clubs. Those kinds of complaints are valid! Probably most beginning journalists in the country—print or electronic—have had to do their share of those kinds of stories and have detested every one of them. Those stories have nothing to do with journalism. They are merely puff pieces. The alternatives for the journalist are to either convince management not to use the news department in that manner or to quit.

For years the farewell address to the graduating students at the Columbia Graduate School of Journalism included a a reminder to start saving a "go-to-hell" fund—a personal nest egg precisely for those occasions when they felt management was making unreasonable or unethical demands. The reasoning behind such a fund is obvious: It's hard to quit when you're broke, even if your professional instincts say you should.

Obviously, it is hard for a beginner to have an idea of which is best, network or local, until he or she has had a chance to make a personal sampling. But one can make some educated guesses based on an honest self-evaluation of personal goals and desired lifestyle. No matter which course is decided upon, an adequate period of self-preparation and of acquiring experience is unavoidable. Once that is out of the way, some courses of action should become rather clear.

For the person convinced that the network is the only place to be, a reasonable immediate goal would be to get a job at one of the network's O&O's. An O&O offers a better chance for taking part in some network productions. It also offers a better chance for someone at the network to recognize one's talents.

For the person who decides against a network job, the

search should be directed toward a good local station—one concerned about news—in a community in which one wants to live. Remember that the freedom of choosing the community in which one wants to live is one of the benefits of local station employment.

In any case, careers have a way of taking care of themselves. Absolutely unforseen opportunities present themselves. The worst thing a beginner can do is to worry about the next step until the present step is out of the way. Whether one works at the local or network level, the ultimate goal, obviously, is to have fun at what one is doing *now*—wherever it is.

8

The Importance
of Who's Boss

In the preceding chapter I discussed some of the options and preferences to consider in pursuing a career in broadcast journalism. At the time it occurred to me that another important consideration rarely discussed is Who's boss? What kind of employer should a young person look for? The beginner at the lower end of the totem pole is likely to have many superiors, but certain organizations simply attract and hold better kinds of management than others. That is important.

There are two distinct levels of management in broadcast news. On the first level there is almost always someone who has the title of news director, even in the smallest news operation. At the network, there are news managers, vice presidents in charge of various news divisions, and a president of network news. Presumably those executives understand the value of news and share the concerns of the working journalists.

The other level of management concerns the owners, whether they are the sole owners of a local station or major powers in the corporate structure of broadcasting. Managers at this level almost never come out of the field of journalism. That does not matter as long as they, too, believe in news. Some do not. And whether it's a network or a local station, behind *every* good news operation there is good management at the ownership level.

The ability to make the right managerial decisions is a talent in itself. From a distance it would appear that the networks are best suited to recruit the best managerial talent and to maintain successful news departments. It is not necessarily true. Looking to the past, network news operations—like the smallest local stations—have risen and fallen on the talents and commitment of a small number of people who are not journalists. Here is how the late Edward R. Morrow, CBS newscaster, described the circumstance:

> . . . the top management of the networks, with a few notable exceptions, has been trained in advertising, research, sales, or show business. But, by the nature of the corporate structure, they also make the final and crucial decisions having to do with news and public affairs.
>
> Frequently they have neither the time nor the competence to do this. It is not easy for the same small group of men to decide whether to buy a new station for millions of dollars, build a new building, alter the rate card, buy a new western, sell a soap opera, decide what defensive line to take in connection with the latest Congressional inquiry, how much money to spend on promoting a new program, what additions or deletions should be made in the existing covey or clutch of vice presidents and at the same time—frequently on the same long day—to give mature, thoughtful consideration to the manifold problems that confront those who are charged with the responsibility for news and public affairs.

Going about the country, one encounters various local stations whose news departments are perenially floundering.

Over the years, management keeps changing the lineup—hiring and firing anchormen, news directors, anybody they they can think of to hire or to fire. The problem in such cases rarely has anything to do with journalism. It has to do with management. The problem is self-perpetuating, of course, because management never fires itself. There are several kinds of bad owners/managers:

- Managers who expect their news departments to cover news without spending money
- Managers who feel supporting the news department means only providing the money
- Managers who see news as just another program to be judged solely by its ratings

Those managers have one thing in common: They do not see the intrinsic value of a good news operation. They have a difficult time accepting the fact that a good news operation will cause them more trouble than a bad one—*trouble* in the sense of having to deal with and protect the news department from the outrage of powerful forces whose toes get stepped on by an aggressive news department. A manager has to believe in what his news department is doing to take that kind of heat. That is why there must be a good manager behind every good news department. In short. it is the role of management to provide a setting for news personnel to do their best work. Good management provides leadership in four broad areas:

- Budgets
- Air time
- Moral support
- Administrative justice

The need for adequate budgets is obvious. Arriving at that goal is easier said than done. A news department always wants more money; more money for staff salaries, more money for facilities, more money for the extra people and equipment that allow one operation to cover more areas in greater depth in order to beat the competition.

For the owner or corporation president who has to decide how to allot the money, it can be a frustrating experience. A given number of dollars never assures an immediate advance in the ratings or an increased level of efficiency. The question of how much to spend is something the manager plays by ear. He makes decisions based on the best advice available. The bookkeepers in the business office always will advise that the news department is spending too much; the news department will always complain it gets too little. Furthermore, the decision-making process is by no means limited to figuring out how much money to spend. It goes far deeper than that.

The amount of air time to grant to the news department is an arbitrary decision. A good old movie rerun will get better ratings than a news program, any time. Therefore, giving the news department generous amounts of air time can be expensive if profit is a station owner's only motive. Not giving a news department sufficient air time can defeat it.

There is the constant problem of keeping up with technology. Again on the best advice available, it is up to the man with the money to decide what is necessary and what is merely frosting. New technology comes and goes; some machines should be bought, some bypassed. The good manager must know what he's doing, he must have very good advice, and he must have very good instincts when those other two categories come up short.

Moral support for the news department is often the hardest and most thankless task of the manager. Fending off self-interested critics is as old as journalism. Fending off those who want to use a news department is equally demanding. It is up to the manager to say no to advertisers, friends, relatives, and politicians who go over the news director's head; that is, to the owners, to try to get the journalists to do something they do not think is right. A news department is under constant pressure. It cannot be wound up and then set aside to run quietly like an expensive clock.

Nowhere is that more true than in the field of administrative justice. It is, ultimately, up to the manager to see that merit is rewarded as a matter of company policy. It is up to him to abide by the fact that once-reliable personnel can become less reliable with age, exhaustion, or boredom—that newcomers *can* succeed and must be given an opportunity. Finally, it is the manager who becomes the court of last resort when an employee feels he or she is being unfairly punished or fired.

It is up to the journalist to be aware that management is not any more constant than anything else human. Broadcast operations are bought, sold, or traded all the time. Networks get new managers. Stations make more or less money from year to year. Profits should not—but usually do—influence the operation of a news department.

There is, however, a certain constancy to the basic precepts of journalism. Certain practices are right or ethical; other practices are not. For the beginner, those precepts must be learned, but it does not end there. Keeping one's footing and searching out news operations where those precepts are *best* practiced is the journalist's best answer to management's rights. Sometimes that means, simply, that the journalist who doesn't like what's going on in a particular station must quit and move on to an operation more in keeping with his or her standards.

9

The Chances for
Women and Minority
Group Members

Although nobody seemed to recognize it for a long time, the lack of opportunities for women and minority group members in broadcasting were very similar. Women, of course, are not a minority group in this country, but they are treated as such. Even today, the chances for women in broadcast journalism are not as good as they are for men. But that's not all that unusual. The chances for women in banking or accounting or law or politics or even teaching are not as good as they are for men, either.

Ironically enough it was the minorities. particularly blacks, who recognized and tried to do something collectively about their minimal roles in radio and television much sooner than women. Most of the women fighting to get their heels in the newsroom doors were white, middle class, and far more inclined to accept the system. Women with college degrees had been conditioned to the fact that when it came to job-hunting, the first question they were asked was, "Do you type?"

Blacks were too long excluded from the system to accept it. As the nation went through the civil rights upheaval in the 1960s, the absence of black reporters on the air was too painfully obvious. But women had not yet faced squarely their discrimination during that period. There were no feminist groups singing "We Shall Overcome" in the earlier part of the 1960s.

So it was in the second half of the 1960s that specific pressure groups were formed to force broadcasters to hire more members from racial minorities. They were somewhat successful. Broadcasters are licensed by the government and are sensitive to organized pressure. Those groups are still in operation and have won formal hiring agreements with stations across the country.

The inequity of women's positions in broadcasting runs deep into the fabric of American society; it has a lot to do with the overall paradoxical position of women in this country who hold much of the wealth in their names but very little of the power. By the late 1960s women had over two-thirds of all the savings accounts. Of all listed securities, 57 percent of them were held in women's names. Three-fourths of the suburban homes were held in women's names. Women have more than half of all the cash in this country (they do most of the shopping). In other words, whether for tax, business, or convenience purposes, they hold the wealth—but in name only.

In 1960 such national statistics did not pertain to minorities. Not only did they lack wealth, they had no power, either. But they had a strong moral argument that was powerfully thrust before the nation. As society and broadcasters began to turn around and to recognize (if not fully admit) racial exclusion, employers started to recruit minorities. And that presented a problem in journalism circles.

Suddenly there was not enough journalistic talent available —at least not enough fully qualified and experienced minority members to go around. In 1972, for example, the American Society of Newspaper Editors reported that less than 1 percent of the nation's newspaper reporters were black. Newspapers had been a traditional training ground for broadcast journalists in the 1960s. The idea was to hire newspaper journalists and to train them in the ways of broadcasting. But trained minority members weren't around. Blacks and Chicanos and Puerto Ricans rarely went into journalism because opportunities were so limited.

A vigorous kind of quiet competition developed for those minority members who were available. Many blacks found it somewhat amusing. They were being courted by the same employers who had turned them down ten years earlier. They were being offered substantial sums of money by one broadcast employer trying to steal them from another.

To a degree, that competition goes on. Quite obviously it exceeds the boundaries of the broadcast industry. Corporations and sundry professional schools are competing actively for qualified or promising minority members. The recruitment is necessary in many fields because minorities have been too long excluded and have become profoundly suspicious of traditionally white American endeavors.

In that sense, then, opportunities for minority group members in broadcasting have been expanding rapidly. The shortage of qualified minority group members has even caused the creation of a relatively new thing in broadcasting—official training programs.

News organizations always have had some sort of training programs, but more often than not they were casual kinds of arrangements whereby a young person with promise was taken in and shown the ropes. The broadcast networks and large local stations were not forced into setting up those kinds of programs because they always had the luxury of picking up personnel from smaller stations. They had the luxury of hiring from among those who had already learned their skills at someone else's expense. That was not possible when it came to minority group members because nobody was training them.

Minority group member has become a kind of code phrase for *black,* but the problem is by no means limited to blacks.

Up to 1972 there had been very few members of *any* identifiable minority group (Mexican, Indian, Puerto Rican, etc.). Even the Jews, who have always had a strong management position in the industry, were rarely on-air news personalities. Furthermore, Jews who were on the air often felt it necessary to change their names. That trend, fortunately, appears to be over. It is possible, however, to get an idea of what has been going on simply by running over the names of those who were or are prominent in broadcast news: Murrow, Huntley, Cronkite, Brinkley, Reasoner, Smith, Reynolds, Edwards, Wallace, Chancellor, McGee, Blair, and so on.

After a point, ethnic nose-counting can become ridiculous. For example, in 1972, a reported advertisement placed by the Department of Judaic Studies at the State University in Albany, New York, for a biblical scholar asked for someone who should be either: "female, black, American-Indian, Spanish surnamed or Oriental." Looking at broadcasting, one presumably could ask, How many Italians are on the air? How many Poles? How many Greeks? The point is that for many years certain easily identifiable ethnic or racial groups were not hired or were not considered for the top jobs.

It would be nice to say all that is a thing of the past, like the bus station restrooms in the South that used to be labeled "colored" or "whites only." Obviously, racial exclusion and segregation have not disappeared in this country, but in broadcasting, one's racial background is no longer an automatic barrier. A significant number of broadcast operations have put an emphasis on hiring and training minority members. They are going to continue to do so because what they do (or do not do) in that field is so highly visible.

Who is to say that there is not still an element of tokenism about it all—that a black or Puerto Rican on the air is not all too often seen as a "black" instead of just another professional? But that is something only time will change, and in practice today, any minority group member who has the abil-

ity and determination can get hired in the broadcasting industry. In other words, no minority group member will be excluded automatically because of his or her racial background.
It is still true, however, that certain parts of the country offer
more opportunity than others.

White middle class women faced a more subtle series of
barriers. Nobody was throwing them out of restaurants or
restrooms. There was no policy to exclude them from positions of real power or influence in broadcasting. It was more
a circumstance of no policy at all. Quite simply, they were
not taken seriously. It was, therefore, much harder to launch
a movement. How do you protest not being taken seriously?
A movement now has been launched, of course, but not before
an awful lot of time was spent in so-called consciousness
raising sessions to make women aware that they are being
discriminated against. Blacks always knew that. For them it
was more a question of what they were going to do about it
and who was going to do it?

For years women have had bylines in respected journalistic
circles, but the truth is, for a long time journalism did not
know what to do with women. Newsrooms were stereotyped
as places where sweaty, whiskey-drinking, poker-playing men
chewed cigars and shouted at copy boys; journalism was no
place for a lady.

Those women who did achieve prominence in the field almost always did it the indirect way, usually breaking into
hard news from the proofreading bench or the society page.
Even then, those who succeeded never were fully accepted
into the fraternity. Working women journalists, for example,
were barred from the Washington Press Club until enormous
pressure was brought upon the male members in the 1970s.
Many of those same male members, incidentally, made their
careers writing about civil rights. There remain many press
clubs across the country from which women are barred or in
which they are decidedly unwelcome.

The myths about women being unsuited for journalism have become increasingly difficult to sustain because today there are women in virtually every major editorial room in the country, but they are not managing editors. Not many, at least. Women who run newspapers usually own them.

Women are not usually broadcast news producers, either. There has *never* been a woman who held an acknowledged key position in the daily decision-making process of a nightly network news broadcast. There are many women presently working in broadcast news, but they have not yet surfaced in many positions of administrative power.

There are a small number of women correspondents in all of the networks. Some receive rather high degrees of publicity and adulation, but within the inner councils, none has much weight. Equally revealing is the fact that there has been little raiding—one network stealing another's female news talent.

Up to a certain point, then, a number of women broadcast journalists have emerged in good and relatively well-paid jobs. At the full producer or editor level they thin out. At the top there is none. Why?

If there were a widespread demand for women journalists on the air, they would be there. Broadcasters live by ratings. They are extraordinarily sensitive to the shifting tastes and viewing habits of their audiences. The public has not demanded women reporters. Women have not demanded women reporters, although surveys show that more women than men listen to the radio and watch television. One may argue that not enough women have been given a chance, that the public has not been allowed to develop a demand for female correspondents because they don't see enough of them. The argument has validity, but it's not that simple. It has to do with the role of women in our society. The approach of journalism toward women has been remarkably similar to society's overall approach toward women: *condescending.*

Here, for example, are some excerpts from a current and presumably successful high school textbook (five printings with revisions) on journalism.

A knowledge of radio and television audience demands is necessary for the simple reason that stations, like other businesses, must recognize the likes and dislikes of their customers. . . .

Sex of probable audience is important because men and women often display sharply different interests. Consequently, program offerings must be arranged accordingly. Newscasts, for example, are more likely to be composed of straight news and sports in the early morning and evening because of the probability of many men listeners. Women's news (*fashions, shopping tips, etc.*) are best suited to the midmorning and afternoon because of the probability of many women listeners. Thus, sex is a distinct influence. . . .

The important caution is to recognize the women's viewpoint. Consequently, stations often employ a woman to gather, prepare and deliver the material. A second important consideration is that of novelty. Like devotees of most fields, the woman is a specialist in fashions, foods and other items concerning the home and her sex in general, and she does not want to hear facts she already knows —she wants something new and interesting. . . . [Author's italics]

Also revealing for me was a conversation I had with a female network associate producer. I asked her why she thought women had not become a force as on-air news reporters.

"I don't think I believe them as much," she said. I do not think her position is a minority view, even among women in the industry. It is a question of conditioning and credibility. A woman telling *her* about strikes and wars and politics and football was not as believable as a man.

It is an important point. A good reporter does not concentrate so much on projecting himself as on projecting his report. The reporter is a transmitter of facts who says what he has to say with authority and credibility. But broadcast newswomen, apparently, are not accepted that way. As one psychologist put it, "They are evaluated only as females, not as persons."

Traveling across the country and looking at local news presentations, one comes across women hosting morning women's programs—almost always, it seems cohosted by nice-looking men—and in the evening one meets the "weather gal." The weather gal is television's counterpart to the society page reporter. It has become acceptable for a woman to tell the audience about the weather but not the war. Odds are she knows more about the war than she knows about cumulus clouds. I have seen women weather reporters conclude their reports by stepping toward the camera and showing off their clothes, telling the viewers that their fashions for the day came from the local dress store or that their hair was styled by the corner beauty shop, which was either sponsoring the weather segment or doing her hair for a free plug on the air. More conditioning . . . more stereotypes.

In such circumstances women are neither seen nor presented as reporters; rather they are "evaluated only as females. . . ."

In a March 15, 1971, *New York* magazine article by Winnie Stork, aptly titled, "Television's Femininity Gap," one network executive (who wisely requested anonymity) was quoted this way:

> Just going by appearance, it is harder for a woman to project an unclassifiable image. Put a

man in a conservative suit and he passes for John Doe. But what makes a woman look like Jane Doe? We have even categorized women by the colour of their hair—the dumb blonde and the bookworm brunette with glasses. It is not just tokenism that has put black women, such as local TV reporters . . . on the screen. Among our batch of prejudices, we seem to believe that all black women look alike —less classifiable. Appearances aside, the women on television seem to be packaged like cigarettes— king size and super king. Never regular. They are exaggerations. They are either very dumb (Goldie Hawn, Dodie Goodman), very beautiful (Eva Gabor, Candice Bergan), very grotesque (Nancy Walker, Martha Raye), or very serious (Gloria Steinem, Marya Mannes, Barbara Walters). And God help the performer who tells the audience, "I'm intelligent." Intelligence must be expressed in a disarming way.

Generalities about the woman's role in broadcast journalism are dangerous if only because they focus too tightly on one brightly lit field. As suggested earlier, what is true in journalism generally has been true in virtually every field (outside of motherhood) in our society. In 1971, for example, for every 100 physicians in this country only 7 were women. Out of every 100 lawyers, only 3 were women, only 1 percent of the federal judges are women, and, of course, no woman has ever sat in the U. S. Supreme Court. Even women teachers have been paid less and promoted less often than their direct male counterparts.

The opportunities for women, as with minority group members, are improving. The question is: How much? Another question is, *Why* are they improving now?

Principally it's a question of awareness. It may be reluctant, but society's attitude toward women is changing. This includes how women view themselves.

A women's magazine in 1973 cites a survey taken as recently as 1969 in which 95 percent of the working women surveyed earned less than men with the same skills (an average of $3,000 a year less). And yet only 8 percent "of the interviewed women believed themselves to be victims of discrimination."

Times do change. Today it is hardly a liberal position to argue that women should receive equal pay for equal work. It seems amusing now that it was once even an argument— but it took a federal law to back it up, and it is still not universally enforced in this country. But as awareness grows and widens and as society changes, so will broadcasting's employment practices. The industry has not been and will not be in the vanguard of social change, but it cannot afford to be in the rear, either.

The August 30, 1971, issue of *Newsweek,* for example, had a report on the following trends:

> In Boston in 1967, two network affiliates had only one woman news reporter between them; four years later, they had five.

> In Houston in 1971, all three network affiliates had at least one woman reporter, two years before that they had none.

> In Washington in 1971, the five television stations had a total of eleven women reporters; all but three of them had been hired since 1969.

Hardly a social revolution, to be sure. But the position of women in broadcast news is still better than it is for women in the rest of the broadcasting industry; that is, better than for women in broadcasting sales or administration or managerial production positions outside of news.

In late 1972, a respected survey of almost all television stations in the country revealed that three out of every four women working in TV had only clerical jobs. In New York 20 to 25 percent of the local stations' employees are women, mostly clerical. But that three-out-of-four "clerical" figure pertains to all television jobs held by women, not just those jobs held by women in the news departments. In news, the percentage of women in merely clerical jobs is not that high. Male desk assistants do much of the clerical work. Women who have made it into the news department with a lot of drive and some competitive credentials (a college degree but no journalism experience, for example) can work themselves out of the purely secretarial roles.

At the network level it is not all that much better for men, either. Young men who come with no more than a college background usually are not going to go anywhere for some time. Increasingly, women who come to the news department with meaningful journalism backgrounds or advanced training in news do not start as secretaries. A young man today still has a better chance of getting into a managerial training program in some money-making business concern, but that is not necessarily true in broadcast news.

That does not mean women are getting into positions of real power in any great numbers. And the continuing level of impatience over women's roles in broadcast news is predictable. Women can see what's going on simply by looking at what's going on the air. When it comes to broadcasting, the news division is one of the few places where a woman can get on the air without having to be a silly comedienne or super intellectual.

Women recognized long ago that the big cities were more open to their career aspirations. For years small stations across the country never hired women reporters. It was an attitude that changed slowly. Once it began to change, the women were not there, because they never had been welcomed in the past. The manager of a rather small local station told me that up until 1971 he had never had a woman even apply personally for a job in his five-man news department. He claimed he hired the first one that did, but, he added, he wouldn't go out looking for one.

In the big cities, then, the broadcast employer always has had the advantage. The supply of educated women willing to take menial jobs in broadcasting (or publishing or advertising, for that matter) has always exceeded the demand. There always has been an abundant supply of researchers and production assistants and newsroom secretaries. That has not always been disastrous for the women who took those jobs, either. A survey indicates, for example, that 66 percent of the present female CBS executives and administrators began as secretaries and clerks. That was the only way they could get in. That may not be fair or enlightened, but that's how things were.

Again, times are changing. As pressure from the feminist movement slowly mounted, the search for genuinely qualified women in broadcast news widened. As the search widened, the supply dwindled. And there you have one of the greater ironies of the present day—that it is in the higher paying prestige (even glamorous) jobs that there are some of the best opportunities for meaningful employment for women. Do not misunderstand. I am not talking about a great number of prestige positions. There are never a large number of great jobs open for anyone, men or women, but as I write this today, I know of two networks that are actively looking for women correspondents and another one that hired five in the past year. I would wager that if even an unknown but otherwise fully qualified, talented, and accomplished female news correspondent made the rounds of the three networks today, she would be hired. And the job would pay her at least

$25,000 to start. The salary would be less, but the same circumstance holds true if that same woman were making the rounds of the major local stations in the country.

The strings attached are the words *qualified* or *accomplished*. It is the old theater story: You can't get in a Broadway play unless you belong to the union, and you can't get into the union unless you are in a play. In the case of broadcasting, the newcomer can get into the union, but the newcomer obviously cannot start out qualified and accomplished. It takes time and determination and drive to succeed. Once the woman is qualified, getting a good job in broadcast news is not that difficult. (Although, of course, the question of what is good is always relative.) Opportunities are opening up and will continue to open up as long as women keep up the pressure.

At ABC in New York, for example, a small group of women from different divisions of the company began meeting informally in 1972. In the beginning they felt it necessary to keep their meetings secret, but within a year the leaders of the group were posting their meeting schedules on the company's bulletin boards with no trouble. One immediate result of their sessions came when they convinced the company to publicly post all job openings as they developed so that the women who were qualified would have the opportunity to apply for them.

In early 1974, CBS appointed three women as directors of women's programs to work as full-time counselors to the women in the company. They handle women employees' gripes and watch out for women's interests in the routine corporate shuffles.

In 1973 women at both ABC and NBC filed formal charges of job discrimination. They brought their complaints to the New York City Commission on Human Rights, the Federal Employment Opportunities Commission, and the U.S. Department of Labor. They may not win anything immediately, but their pressure is obvious.

Clearly it is still not as easy for a woman to get a start, to get equal pay, or to go as far as a male colleague. Compared to past decades, however, it is certainly easier. Moreover, working in the industry, one senses a new mood. One comes across more and more women working in decent jobs not only at the network level but also at local stations where they would not even have been considered five or six years ago. Perhaps more significant than the actual number of jobs being filled by women is the fact that one senses also that the women employed are being accepted as *persons*.

10

Broadcast Unions

The idea of joining a union may be one of the last things you think of in planning a broadcast news career, but if you decide to go beyond the boundaries of a small local station, you cannot avoid the question of unions. Sooner or later, everyone in the electronic media works with people from several different broadcast unions. Whether a person is required to join a union depends on the individual station.

Most radio and television stations in the smaller and even medium-sized cities are nonunion. Virtually all stations in the major markets have signed bargaining agreements with the unions.

Broadcast unions are divided along lines of jurisdiction. Each job falls under a specific jurisdiction controlled by a union. Jurisdictions are what unions fight about a lot among themselves.

For example, the technicians who record sound at ABC network radio news are members of the National Association of Broadcast Employees and Technicians (NABET). They record and edit news interviews, and their jobs are under NABET's jurisdiction. The technician who records sound for television news film cameras, on the other hand, is a member of the International Alliance of Theatrical Stage Employees and Moving Picture Machine Operators (IATSE). Sound-on-film recording, then, is under IATSE's jurisdiction. If the

NABET or IATSE technician ever tries to move into the other's jurisdiction, there's trouble.

Job jurisdictions are negotiated with management. The employers may not like having to deal with unions, but they have no choice, since the right of working people to join unions or to organize themselves into labor organizations is guaranteed by law. Once the unions have won bargaining agreements, management is required to deal with them.

Many young people coming into broadcasting find their early brushes with union jurisdiction frustrating. They may be coming from small stations where they did everything: appeared on the air, ran the radio studio, edited tape, and operated the film cameras. As they move to bigger, union organized stations, that no longer is possible. One can do those jobs only if one is in the right union.

The unions may appear to be limiting opportunities for beginners. As mentioned in an earlier chapter, promising young desk assistants cannot be given the opportunity to do a quick story on the air now and then because they are not in the proper union. If they do join the union, then management must pay them the minimum union wages, which will be far in excess of a desk assistant's normal pay. Management will not do that. It's too expensive. In the beginning, then, the whole system may seem unfair or too restrictive. But it is necessary to understand the reasons for the growth of the union movement in broadcasting which counted about 350,000 members in and outside broadcasting by the early 1970s.

I have always been puzzled by how little is known about the broadcast unions outside of the industry itself—puzzled only because of the immense influence the unions have on broadcasting. When a longshoremen's labor leader threatens, Congress listens. When a new Teamster president is elected, he makes headlines and magazine covers. The only time broadcast unions get into the press is when they strike, and even then, the issues don't seem to make much sense to the public.

In the beginning broadcasting had no influence. When radio started in the early 1920s, the whole thing was really an experiment. Radio stations didn't make any money then. They were subsidized, generally, by newspapers or manufacturers. Westinghouse, for example, bankrolled the first station in Pittsburgh in 1920 because the company wanted to sell radio sets.

Because the industry was such a profitless infant in the 1920s, broadcast employees were paid little. Many performers and writers got nothing—no pay. The late columnist Heywood Broun wrote in 1924, "These broadcasters do not pay. Instead they offer the performer publicity. It is a highly depreciated currency."

So in the beginning, there was very little the employees could do other than accept whatever management offered. By 1926–1927, the NBC radio network was created. CBS came about a year later. Mutual Broadcasting was put together in 1934. By then, radio was making money. Even at the height of the depression, both NBC and CBS were showing profits in the $1 million range. The employees, however, still weren't making much.

There are many old-timers still around who remember some of the outrageous working conditions they had to accept. They would be asked to come in at 8:00 A.M. to record a radio program and then be sent home for several hours before returning that evening to put the program on the air. They were not paid for those intervening hours. That was a split shift.

There were engineers who worked at the radio station's transmitter up on a hill or on the top of a building. In addition to doing all the engineering chores, they also worked as the announcers, reading on the air the occasional commercial announcements sent up by the owners.

Everyone from those early years can tell similar stories.

The point is the unions were formed and grew strong because they were needed. Few people got rich because of union membership, but many got fair wages and reasonable working conditions only because of union organization.

Also, it is important to recognize the times in which the broadcast unions were born. In the 1920s and early 1930s the labor movement was still fighting for a right to exist. In Europe getting the Holy See to affirm the right of Catholics to belong to unions required heavy lobbying. Industrial barons saw organized labor as some sort of communism.

It was not until the legislation of Roosevelt's New Deal era that the picture changed dramatically. The Wagner Act, establishing the National Labor Relations Board (NLRB), was not passed until 1935, and it was not until 1938 that Congress passed a federal minimum wage—25 cents an hour! The major labor movement in broadcasting rode the tide of that kind of new legislation. It grew immensely with the coming of television, but television's prominence was considerably delayed because of World War II, when manufacturing priorities were switched to building war machines.

For example, as early as 1937 there were seventeen experimental television stations in operation. In 1939 there were live television broadcasts (predictably, a major league baseball game, a college football game, and a boxing match). Then the war struck, and television stalled. It was not until 1950 that the first presidential message to Congress was carried on the networks, and not until 1966 that the first presidential message was carried live by the networks in color. It was only in the mid-1950s that television news became a significant entity, and at that time it was very crude, indeed.

In the beginning no one had a clear idea of where broadcasting was going as it grew up. For that matter, it is still growing, and so is the process of labor organization within the industry.

Today, the broadcast journalist deals principally with six major unions. None of these unions is involved solely with news. Members of the various unions work on other kinds of program of outside news, but these are the unions one deals with to one degree or another in the process of news production:

- The American Federation of Radio and Television Artists (AFTRA)
- The Writers Guild, east and west (WGA)
- The Directors Guild of America (DGA)
- The International Alliance of Theatrical Stage Employees and Moving Picture Machine Operators (IATSE)
- The National Association of Broadcast Employees and Technicians (NABET)
- The International Brotherhood of Electrical Workers (IBEW)

The first three unions generally include editorial employees rather than technicians, and the second three represent more the employees who actually run the machines and equipment of broadcasting.

News writers and reporters come under the jurisdiction of two organizations: WGA and AFTRA. If a broadcast station has bargaining agreements with AFTRA or WGA, a new employee hired at that station is required to apply for membership within thirty days.

The Writers Guild

Up to the early 1950s there were at least five different organizations involved in broadcast writing (screen writers, radio writers, television writers). In 1954 there was a merger between the radio writers and the screen writers. What came out of the merger was the WGA, divided by the Mississippi River to form WGA east and west.

The WGA is not affiliated with the AFL–CIO. It is an independent union. In fact, many writers do not think of themselves as union members. They think of themselves as guild members banded together for common cause.

For the news writer, the WGA bargains with the station or the network for minimum staff salaries. The union has secured a standard set of additional fees for certain kinds of programs or for editing responsibilities. The WGA also has secured job seniority protection, limited just causes for dismissal, reasonable working conditions, and the usual pension, welfare, holiday, and vacation benefits.

Those kinds of things are secured by the writers bargaining as one group with management. The pay scales, or guaranteed minimums, vary from region to region. The scales move upward after each new contract is negotiated. Generally, a contract runs for three years. Broadcast news writers frequently complain about their union. Part of that is because the WGA is not as powerful or as militant as the technicians' unions. Part of that is because writers do not make as much money as persons who appear on the air. And part of that is because newsmen do not fit comfortably in any union. In fact, the WGA offers its members better job security benefits than the performers' union.

The American Federation of Radio and Television Artists

AFTRA (pronounced as it is spelled) was formed and grew strong when radio was king. As a labor organization, it traces its roots back directly to broadcasting. It began as the American Federation of Radio Artists (AFRA) in 1937. In 1952, once television obviously was here to stay, they added a *T* to AFRA and expanded it to include performers in the television medium.

AFTRA was never envisioned as a union for news people. It was, and is, essentially a union for free-lance performers— people who appear on entertainment programs and do commercials. It is known as a talent union.

Broadcast news people came into AFTRA because they

had no other place to go. They were on the air and AFTRA was the most appropriate union to represent what they did for a living. But news people in AFTRA membership have always been a distinct minority. It is ironic that the first (and only) nationwide AFTRA strike was over local AFTRA news people.

The alliance between news people and entertainers is not an easy one. The news people do not fit easily in AFTRA, but they have little option except to form their own organization. The problem with that is that the news people need the strength of the whole union behind them when it comes time for bargaining with management. A strike by news people isn't going to mean much unless everyone in AFTRA goes out with them—Johnny Carson, Captain Kangaroo, the soap opera performers, etc. Also, AFTRA, unlike the Writers Guild, is affiliated with the AFL–CIO and has that organization's huge weight and expertise behind it.

Journalists do not fit easily in AFTRA because being on the air is not the most important function of a news person. First one must be a journalist. The journalist covers a story and then appears on television or radio because that's where his or her reports are done, but it is merely the last step in the journalistic process.

Broadcast journalists usually are full-time employees. Entertainers are not. Yet AFTRA is principally a union for free-lance artists. Technicians in broadcasting often tease reporters about their union. The technicians see AFTRA as more of a country club than a powerful labor organization.

When it comes to hard-nosed bargaining and labor-management relations, it is true that WGA and AFTRA members are not in the same league as the technicians and engineers. But many broadcast news personnel negotiate their own personal contracts for wages and fees far above the union scale. Technicians do not do that. Whatever the union negotiates is what they get paid.

Like every other union, AFTRA does bargain with management for minimum wage scales for its members. Unlike other unions, however, AFTRA is exceedingly concerned with fees paid to its members. Performers traditionally receive talent fees when they appear on the air. News people in the networks and at major local stations receive these fees every time their faces, names, or voices are used. That is rather silly since news people are full-time employees and are paid a weekly base wage, or guarantee.

The fee system was designated for the free-lance performer, but since news people are in AFTRA, the fee system was grafted onto their agreements with management. Once a news person's guarantee reaches a certain level, fees are no longer paid. In 1974, that level was $40,000 a year. News people in the majority of local stations outside the major cities are not paid fees. Instead, they receive only a weekly wage.

Because of the unstable nature of the performer's world, AFTRA never has been able to secure for its performers or news people any kind of meaningful job protection. There is no seniority system, and most employees under AFTRA contracts can be fired by management without much trouble. That's the way it has always been in the entertainment world, and AFTRA is part of that world.

That is not true for the technicians. Firing a union technician with seniority can be very difficult, indeed. The technician in the broadcast industry is distinguished by two factors: his or her technical skill, and membership in a strong union.

International Alliance of Theatrical Stage Employees and Moving Picture Machine Operators

Reporters and writers in television often work with members of IATSE (pronounced I-yaht-see). In the networks, the newsreel camera person and the lighting and sound recording technicians all are members of IATSE. Photography and film editing most often are under IATSE's jurisdiction, although there are regional exceptions where the jurisdiction has been won by another union. Only 10 percent of the broadcasting stations in this country have bargaining agreements with IATSE, but they are the major ones.

Basically IATSE is a movie production and projectionists' union. It grew up with the movie industry, but it was formed before the turn of the century as a stagehand's union. Originally membership was restricted to carpenters, electricians, and propertymen in theatrical stage productions. One had to have a particular stage craft to get in.

Today, it is still an exceedingly difficult union to get into in big cities and major production areas such as New York, Los Angeles, Chicago, and Washington. There really is no other union like IATSE in broadcasting. It was always a "family union," or what is known as a father-and-son union. That means one gets in almost automatically if one's father is in the union and stands a good chance of getting in if one's uncle or father-in-law is an active member. In the big cities it is very difficult to get into without connections, union supporters, or powerful reasons for admittance. In 1973 an IATSE official in New York was convicted of taking a $10,000 bribe to get a man into the union.

With the growth of movies, the union followed the stage actors and producers into motion pictures. IATSE men learned the crafts of movie production and became enormously powerful. Then came television and that medium's considerable reliance on film. Again, IATSE followed everyone else into television and gained jurisdiction over many of the technical jobs including newsreel production. In effect, almost anything done on film at the networks comes under IATSE's jurisdiction.

Large national unions are broken down into smaller groups known as locals spread across the country. IATSE is made up of roughly 900 locals with 60,000 members in the 50 states, Puerto Rico, and Canada.

There are IATSE locals for every craft connected with film production. A movie producer in Hollywood, for example, conceivably may have to deal with at least twenty different IATSE locals just to make one feature film.

To give you an idea of the skills involved, Hollywood IATSE Local 44 is made up of motion picture studio propertymen, swing gang men, nurserymen, set dressers, propmakers, prop-miniature men, upholsterers, drapers, and special effects men. There is also Local 884, made up of motion picture studio teachers and welfare workers. There are many, many other locals.

There are nowhere near that many locals involved in news production. Where IATSE people are involved in news, however, the categories and craft restrictions are rigid. For example, camera people belong to one IATSE local in New York. Lighting and sound technicians belong to another. Film editors belong to still another—all in the same city. It is probably easiest to remember IATSE simply as the film union. That distinguishes it from the unions that have jurisdiction over other aspects of news production such as those involving video tape and electronic cameras.

In many respects IATSE is similar to AFTRA. It is basically a union for free-lance employees. That makes sense, since most of its members started out working on theatrical and movie productions. Once the movie is made, the work is over, and workers go on to another production. But news production provided a different set of circumstances. Like reporters, staff camera crews and other IATSE members are needed full-time.

Therefore there are two different pay scales. Free-lance workers get paid more for each day because they work fewer days in the year. For example, in 1972, a free-lance camera person working for a news operation in New York got $100 a day. The staff camera person doing the same job received only $74.00.

Over the years IATSE has negotiated elaborate rules and regulations with management concerning working conditions for IATSE members. Everything is specified: how many hours a person can be asked to work, how overtime payments are determined, what cash penalties management must pay to each worker if the rules are broken. Seniority is all-important in IATSE, and every member is protected from being fired or removed without just cause.

In addition to the base wages, IATSE also has negotiated rather elaborate fringe benefits for its members. For example, in 1973, an IATSE contract in New York stipulated that for every hour the IATSE person works, the employer pays $.45 into the union's health and welfare fund. For every full day the person works, management contributes $2.75 toward his or her vacation pay. For the worker's pension, management has to pay into the union's pension fund $.48 for every hour worked. If you add up just those fringe benefits, it comes to nearly $10.00 a day per person.

The National Association of Broadcast Employees and Technicians

NABET (pronounced nay-bet) and AFTRA are the only two unions in the industry that can trace their roots directly to broadcasting. Both came out of radio. As a union, NABET invented itself as it went along and grew with the industry.

NABET started as an informal kind of house union at NBC. It began with a few technicians meeting with members of management to discuss their grievances. But radio was growing too fast for such informality to last. In 1933 the men handling the electronics at NBC formed the Association of Technical Employees (ATE). It was really more of an association than a union, but it survived at NBC and slowly prospered. Other stations were taken into the ATE.

In 1940 the ATE changed its name to the National Association of Engineers and Technicians. By then the union was battling with another labor organization for jurisdiction over certain jobs. Eleven years later the union decided to expand still further and changed its name finally to the National Association of Broadcast Employees and Technicians.

That change signified the fact that NABET was interested in getting as many workers as possible under its umbrella. There are two kinds of unions: vertical unions and horizontal unions. The terms aren't important, but the philosophy behind them is. Horizontal unions are organized along strict craft lines. Plumbers are in a plumbers' union. Carpenters are in a carpenters' union. Vertical unions extend up and down and take in many different kinds of crafts. Therefore, NABET dropped the word *engineers,* replaced it with *employees,* and took in all kinds of job categories. NABET's leaders were looking for strength in numbers. The union also became affiliated with the AFL–CIO.

By the early 1970s, NABET had 8,500 members. Both NBC and ABC networks are in NABET's jurisdiction. (CBS deals with another technicians' union.) NABET is principally a union for electronic technicians. That's where its real membership strength is found. But it also represents many other kinds of crafts.

At the ABC station in San Francisco not only are engineers in NABET but also the station's messengers, switchboard operators, publicists, and the station gardener. NABET even has some editorial employees, such as news producers and writers, under its jurisdiction.

From the outside, it would appear that there is strength in such numbers. There is, but there are also problems. It is hard for the union to bargain with management when it is representing so many different kinds of people. The engineers want one thing, the hairdressers want something else, the messengers want their problems taken care of, and so on.

In trying to deal with these problems, NABET has done two things. First, union negotiators bargain for certain basic working conditions, vacation periods, holidays, fringe benefits, and all the other bread-and-butter issues that concern everyone. Then, the union has divided its members into six different categories, each with different pay scales.

The major category is made up of the men and women with whom the journalist most often works. These are the studio electronic camera people, the video tape machine operators, the radio engineers, tape editors, recording specialists, and so on.

An important difference between IATSE, the film union, and NABET, the engineers' union, is that NABET does not seek free-lance employees. Virtually all NABET members work full-time in broadcasting. They do not work on one production for a few days and then go looking for another production. If management needs additional personnel under NABET's jurisdiction, the employer either hires more full-time employees or pays overtime to the existing employees to do the extra work. Anyone hired by management can get into the union.

NABET does not have the large number of union locals that IATSE maintains. In New York, for example, there are only two NABET locals: one for the employees at ABC and one for the employees at NBC.

International Brotherhood of Electrical Workers

The IBEW was formed before the turn of the century. It began as a union for telegraph wire and linemen. The IBEW is basically an electricians' union. It is a huge union, but only a fraction of the membership works directly in broadcast production. Out of nearly a million members, only about 11,000 work in radio, television, and sound recording. The union's major broadcast strength is in the CBS network and other local radio and television stations.

IBEW engineers do the same thing as NABET engineers. The jobs are the same, only the unions are different. IBEW got into broadcasting in the 1920s and 1930s when broadcast technicians in radio began looking for a union to represent them. IBEW was a powerful union because its members worked in construction, manufacturing, railroad, telephone operations, and any other industry requiring electricians' skills. IBEW, therefore, was a logical choice for the broadcast engineers. Unlike NABET, IBEW sticks pretty much to the crafts directly associated with electronics. It is not a vertical union.

There are only four IBEW job categories in broadcasting. These include technicians, assistant supervisors, technical directors, and supervisors. Like NABET, IBEW is not a freelance union. In fact, IBEW discourages even vacation relief employment. It is allowed in some of the smaller stations but not generally at the network or at its major stations. To avoid employment of vacation reliefers, IBEW members schedule their vacations to insure enough people on the job at any one time. If not, they work overtime. CBS engineers and technicians in New York have individually averaged 300 hours of overtime a year.

NABET and IBEW have similar contracts with the networks when it comes to working conditions. seniority benefits, pay scales, and so on. Also like NABET, a person is taken into the union if hired by the management.

Directors Guild of America

The DGA is a curious union. Legally, it's not even a union. Its members are considered supervisory personnel. That means they are members of management and therefore are not protected by the National Labor Relations Board. It is the most expensive labor organization in the industry. The DGA initiation fee for a director is $2,000.

The DGA came about as a result of a merger in 1960 between the Radio and Television Directors Guild and the Screen Directors Guild. By the early 1970s, the DGA had roughly 3,500 members throughout the country.

As the title suggests, the most important members of the DGA work as directors. There are also other kinds of job categories included in the guild, however—associate directors, stage managers, and production assistants. (PA's do not have to pay $2,000 to get into the DGA, but, of course, they don't get directors' wages, either.)

The DGA does not have locals. It is simply one national organization representing its members throughout the broadcasting and movie industries.

There are all kinds of directors. The range is from famous, eccentric Hollywood movie directors to unknown news documentary directors. Many news writers and producers join the DGA and double as directors. There is a separate fee paid for for each job title on a documentary. Therefore the writer-producer-director receives three fees for one program.

Working journalists come into contact with directors most often in the control rooms. It is the director who directs the studio cameras while a news program is on the air. It is the director who puts the show on the air, pulling together the intricate cues, scripts, film, tape, and live reports. Assisting the director is the associate director (the AD). The other technicians one finds in a network control room, such as the technical director and audio and video technicians, are members of NABET or IBEW. Do not confuse a station's news director, who is boss of the news gathering operation, and the director, who runs the control room.

Without a good director, a news program stumbles. Sometimes a journalist can work days or even weeks on a film report, only to see it flop on the air because the director did something wrong. The director of a live news program has one of the most demanding jobs in all of broadcasting, being a combination technician and creative journalist. Directors must understand both the editorial and the technical fields. If the director loses control, what goes on the air is bound to be a mess.

There is no one way to become a director. Some television directors also work on movies. Most begin as assistants to directors and learn the craft through an apprenticeship.

Stage managers work on the floor of the studio. They wear headsets that allow them to communicate with the talent in the studio and the director in the control room. Stage managers in television frequently are called floor directors, because that's what they do—direct the action on the studio floor. They see that the electronic cameras and other equipment are placed properly. They work directly with the anchor person and other news personnel appearing on the air. They relay cues and messages and generally see to it that the studio is running quietly and efficiently.

Production assistants do what their title implies. They help out in the production of a program. In the curious ways of the industry, PA's at ABC and CBS are members of the DGA; at NBC they are not.

DGA officials are almost aggressively non-union. As one DGA leader in New York put it, "The guild does *not* consider itself a union. We have no shop stewards, no locals, only a national association made up of artisans and craftsmen with no union trappings."

As in many of the other unions discussed, the strength of the DGA membership is not in news. However, the DGA does bargain with management for basic wages for its members. Directors do not receive hourly wages. Most of the important directors in broadcast news negotiate their own contracts with management far above the minimum pay scales. For those below the director, wages are paid on an hourly basis and include overtime payments. Most members of the DGA are free-lance artists. For full-time staff employees, such as those who work in news, there are seniority benefits. The DGA also negotiates for the usual health, welfare, and pension benefits.

Beyond the bread-and-butter issues, however, the DGA gets into far more complicated bargaining. Directors frequently feel victimized by producers (or whoever puts up the money for a production). Therefore, the DGA fights for the directors over such things as credits on the screen and editing rights.

Where Are the Unions Going?

It was only a few years ago that the broadcast unions were going nowhere. They grew merely more rigid, more bureaucratic, more determined to maintain the status quo. The status quo meant very few minority group members and virtually no women except in those jobs that traditionally went to women.

All that is changing. For years the unions fought blindly to protect what they had, to prevent change. That's understandable. The broadcast unions had it good and didn't want anything messing that up. But times change, and change is coming most rapidly in the ranks of the technicians working in broadcast news. Formerly those technical jobs (and the accompanying excellent salaries) were dominated by the white male. They still are, but not exclusively.

Women are getting behind the cameras—something that occurred only rarely even in the early 1970s. For years the huge cameraman's union in New York had only one woman. There were always a few blacks, but their entrance into the union was anything but rapid.

Women always have been accepted in the film editor's ranks but most often as assistants rather than full editors. A major breakthrough came as women got into the fields of sound, lighting, and engineering (principally as video tape machine operators and editors).

No one is saying these newcomers are being widely accepted with enthusiasm. They are getting in as society demands it and as broadcast employers bend to public will. Remember that whatever policies the broadcast union pursued in the past, they did so with the acquiescence of management.

In addition to the changes brought about by social pressure, even greater change is pressing the status quo of the unions as a result of technological innovations. One of the best kept secrets in broadcasting is how relatively unaffected the industry has been by the technology revolution of the 1960s. That sounds ridiculous, I know. After all, broadcasting relies on electronics, and the marvel of electronics is what this computer age is all about. To be sure, broadcasting has been affected by the transistor generation. But the basic gear behind broadcast news production has remained relatively unchanged.

Film and audio tape editing techniques, for example, are primitive when measured by modern technological standards. Studio cameras still are lumbering and horribly expensive. The basic design and internal structure of the 16-millimeter film cameras used in news virtually are unchanged from the first portable sound cameras that came on the market. Video tape machines have been shrunken by the transistor, but they remain notoriously expensive, cranky, and in need of constant attention.

By the 1970s however, automation and simplification of technology began to make their presence felt as never before in the industry. Until then, the trend had been toward more and more manpower. In the decade between 1960 and 1970, the engineering and technical staffs in broadcasting doubled! Now that trend is over.

Fully automated radio stations run by computers with pretaped material are on the air. Computerized video tape editing is in practice. Video tape cartridges are here. Tiny, portable live electronic cameras are used in news production. All of those kinds of innovations require fewer humans to operate them. Those who do must understand how the new gear works. That means a demand for new, better trained technicians to come into the industry as the older members retire.

Understandably, the unions have not been very happy about all this. Unions want to preserve jobs for their members now on the books. A broadcast technician is precisely that—a technician. He understands electronics. He loves the gadgets of the industry. He does not hate the machine as some manual laborer may hate a machine about to take his job. But the technician does mistrust management, and what management may want to do with the machine and his job.

Management is a lot like the technician. American business is fascinated by machines and what they can do. Also, machines don't talk back. They don't demand health insurance or severance pay, and they don't form unions. (At least the computers haven't done so yet!)

The dilemma of automation and simplified technology facing the older established order of technicians provides a widening horizon of opportunity for newcomers who have more advanced. up-to-date training. It will be easier for them to accept the new since they never really knew the old.

There are also major changes destined to come to the basic union structures as they now exist. As the industry changes technologically, the unions cannot remain the same, although they have tried to do so. The truth is, the old jurisdictions cannot stand up.

In the battle of automation and simplification, management always has the advantage. After all, it is up to the management to decide what new gadget to buy, and in the crucial years of the 1960s, it was management that adopted the stronger position in labor negotiations.

That had a lot to do with the way bargaining is done in the broadcast industry. Historically, each union has gone its own separate way, taking on management at the bargaining table by itself. Management recognized the foolishness of that a long time ago. When management sits down to bargain with the unions, for example, all three networks go in together whenever possible. The unions do not. Each has fought for its own interests and has not worried about the rest. That makes for split forces. In an essay on the overall broadcast union structure, Claude McCue, executive secretary of AFTRA's Los Angeles office, put it bluntly:

> The cannibalism among unions in this schizophrenic industry has created a jungle of competition between workers trying to supplant each other. Even if the companies had developed a plan with a blueprint . . . they would not have reaped greater benefits than they do from this voluntary indulgence by the unions of their own appetites.

There are some rare exceptions to the otherwise "cannibal" world. When television began to use film, a battle broke out between the Screen Actors Guild (SAG) and AFTRA. Both unions claimed they had jurisdiction over television entertainment and commercials done on film. The battle went on for years, but in 1958, SAG and AFTRA realized that they had better make peace. Otherwise, management could play one union off against the other. SAG and AFTRA became sister unions. They negotiated jointly. Today, a performer joining one of the unions is required to pay only half the initiation fee to join the other union.

That same sort of alliance makes sense throughout the labor organizations of the broadcast industry. It has not come because the unions simply have not yet awakened to the massive changes about to engulf them.

It is hard to predict how all of these changes will affect the young person coming into the industry. As cities grow larger and local stations expand, it is logical to expect that broadcast labor organizing also will expand. Whatever happens, however, it is likely that the newcomer will have a better chance today working within the union structure than he or she had in the 1950s or 1960s.

11

Future Thoughts
About Broadcasting

Many of us in broadcast news today have been in the industry all of our adult lives. That gives one the feeling that broadcast careers have always been around—like careers in banking or the military. The fact is, radio didn't start until the 1920s. It was hard to take television seriously until the 1950s. Many of our parents were born before there was such a thing as a broadcast career.

The basic precepts of news reporting have been around for a long time. The electronic media is still being invented as we go along. Every year brings some new invention that allows us to do something more in electronic reporting. Soon there will be more satellites whirling over the United States —and the world—allowing broadcasters to vastly expand the number of their channels to the public. There will be informational services on the air twenty-four hours a day.

In New York, at the time of this writing, experiments are being conducted with something I think of as stereo television. In an experiment, the public television station broadcast a program on two channels. To watch it, you lined up two television sets side by side. The same program was shown from two points of view, simultaneously. For example, they showed a ball bouncing from one screen to another.

Actually, something like that goes on all the time in a television control room. When television covers a football game the director sits in a control room facing several monitors. Each monitor shows the picture being fed by a live camera. It's up to the director to decide which of those pictures to put on the air. He is constantly switching from one camera to another. But up to now, he was able to show the viewer at home only one picture at a time. Perhaps someday we will be covering news with several live cameras and feeding two channels and two different views of the same news event at the same time. Of course the viewer would have to have two TV sets, but in America today that's no problem.

Still to come is the full exploration of closed circuit television, and no one knows where cable television is going to lead. Everyone senses, however, that the possibilities are endless. There are dozens of experiments in the works.

A significant segment of young people already are moving into what is described as counter-culture news. Cable television and the avante-garde FM radio stations are beginning to field a number of journalists providing a totally different look at news events of interest to their particular kinds of audiences.

My point is that all of these innovations will dramatically affect the broadcast job market. What has been detailed in this book is how one goes about getting into the rather traditional, established structure of broadcast journalism as it exists now. But the industry is constantly mutating, moving around, changing. For the newcomer, that's good. There is lots of room for new ideas.

A young woman I know, for example, knocked on several broadcast newsroom doors. She had had some experience in broadcasting but couldn't find a job she wanted. So she decided to start her own business. She went to Washington and contacted as many local stations across the country as was reasonable. Her sales pitch to them was that they needed their own reporter in the Capitol. She said she would be available to interview their local congressmen and senators in Washington. She bought a sound camera and a tape recorder and provided news clips to the stations back home—for a fee, of course.

I do not know if she made any money. There is a lot of competition in Washington with similar services, but she was her own boss. She made a lot of contacts, and she had more fun than she would have had working as somebody's secretary.

To the imaginative or adventurous young journalist, what I'm suggesting is that just because things are done in a certain way today does not mean they have to be done that way tomorrow. A major element of journalism is competition. That can extend not only to getting a story first but also to competing in setting up new kinds of news enterprises. The magazine industry is always looking for different kinds of specialized audiences and then designing publications to fit those needs. Of course, it isn't as easy to do in broadcasting. You need more than a printing press and post office privileges. But as broadcast equipment grows smaller, simpler, and more portable, it becomes more possible to create alternatives to what exists today.

Alternatives is a fancy way of saying new jobs. In the years ahead we will see more and more alternatives sprouting up around the present established order of broadcasting. That is particularly true as audience tastes and interests grow more fragmented and specialized.

In short, new ways of doing things are all over the horizon. Realistically speaking, the newcomer probably will have to start in an existing broadcast operation to gain experience.

But, finally, what I'm urging is that one keep in mind not only the potential of jobs that do not yet exist but also the potential for the newcomer to play a part in thinking up those new jobs and helping to create them.

Where to Get Information About Journalism Courses and Radio/Television Stations

The American Council on Education for Journalism (A.C.E.J.) keeps an up-to-date list of schools that offer accredited courses in journalism. One can obtain a free copy of this list by writing to:

Professor Milton Gross
A.C.E.J.
School of Journalism
University of Missouri
Columbia, Missouri 65201

Every year the Association for Education in Journalism publishes a directory of schools offering journalism courses. It comes in the annual edition of *The Journalism Educator,* which can be found in many local libraries.

The National Association of Broadcasters (NAB) tabulates colleges and universities offering courses or degrees in broadcasting. One can obtain that list, free, by writing to:

National Association of Broadcasters
1771 N Street N.W.
Washington, D.C. 20036

The American Society of Journalism School Administrators puts out a comprehensive annual directory describing journalism schools, departments, seminars, and so on. The publication is entitled *The Journalism Educator*. It can be obtained for $3.00 by writing to:

> *The Journalism Educator*
> c/o The School of Journalism
> University of Minnesota
> Minneapolis, Minnesota 55455

Broadcasting Yearbook lists broadcasting news services (organizations that supply news material to stations domestically and overseas), foreign language bureaus, ethnic-oriented news material, and some employment agencies for news personnel, as well as brief fact sketches of every commercial broadcasting operation in the United States, Canada, Mexico, and the Caribbean.

Some local libraries or colleges may receive this annual publication. Most local stations have a copy of the yearbook, or one may puchase a copy by sending $13.00 to:

> *Broadcasting Yearbook*
> 1735 DeSales Steet, N.W.
> Washington, D.C.. 20036

Another good source for information on television and radio stations across the country is a series of books published annually under the title *The Working Press of the Nation*. Included in that series is the *Radio and Television Directory*.

It contains names, addresses, and personnel of the broadcast stations in the United States and Canada. The directory is put out principally for public relations organizations interested in contacting individual stations. The series is published by the National Research Bureau, Inc., Burlington, Iowa. The publication is expensive but may be found in your public library.

Index